DEMYSTIFYING RESEARCH

Demystifying Research

A Primer for Novice Researchers

By

Cynthia L. Jackson
University of the Virgin Islands

and

George R. Taylor
Coppin State University, Maryland, USA

SENSE PUBLISHERS
ROTTERDAM / TAIPEI

A C.I.P. record for this book is available from the Library of Congress.

ISBN 978-90-8790-067-0 (paperback)
ISBN 978-90-8790-068-7 (hardback)

Published by: Sense Publishers,
P.O. Box 21858, 3001 AW Rotterdam, The Netherlands
http://www.sensepublishers.com

Printed on acid-free paper

DEDICATION

The *Primer* is dedicated to the novice researchers with whom we have worked over the years. You taught us about the basic information novice researchers need that experienced researchers take for granted. You encouraged us to share with others what we learned from you.

CONTENTS

CONTENTS

PREFACE

Some of the most fearful and dreaded moments of many graduate learners are beginning their theses or dissertations. Much of the anxiety experienced can be easily and readily reduced when learners are aware that research is a skill that can be acquired. Simply put, you can learn to do research.

This book is an outgrowth of our teaching experiences in graduate level research courses and seminars at Coppin State University, The Union Institute and University, and Nova University. We have found that generally, graduate learners tend to approach scholarly research as some type of mystical journey. They are not sure where research starts and the paths taken to accomplish research objectives.

The *Primer* is written primarily for graduate level producers of education and social science research. It is also appropriate for seniors who are proposing and conducting a research project as a culminating undergraduate requirement, and individual and groups conducting research projects in communities on topics independent of an academic program. The *Primer* is our way to give the novice researcher an informed means of assuming the role of researcher and embarking on a research study. It is written with the encouragement of learners who participated in our research courses and seminars.

As with any undertaking that is based on skill development, the more you use the skill the more adept you become with the skill. The quality and usefulness of all research is only as good as the skills of the researcher and the clarity of the research study.

There are no recipes for conducting research. Research can be ambiguous. The appropriate focus, design, research approach, methodologies, and techniques vary from researcher to researcher, topic to topic, and research setting to research setting. No one can be told how much reading is sufficient, how much thinking is sufficient, how much inquiry is sufficient, and how much writing is sufficient. Sufficient is determined by the researcher and dictated by the research topic, what the researcher wants to understand, the researcher's current knowledge about the topic, and the researcher's research skill level.

Research is also an art form. It should be an intellectual artistic expression of ideas that are articulated powerfully to provoke thought, dialogue, and more research. Yet, as with all art forms there are common characteristics or attributes upon which they are judged. For research, the common characteristics are embedded in the application of the research process. And so, we return to the skills of the researcher.

Through the *Primer* we want to demystify the first phase of the research process - conceptualization and focus. Specific research methodologies are only discussed generally. There is excellent literature available on the application of specific research methodologies and the analysis of the data. Some of them are contained in the bibliography of this book.

The *Primer* is designed to give you insights about the research process and heighten your awareness of the concerns of researchers. It is divided into four parts:

- Part I provides preliminary considerations for a frame of reference about scholarly research and your role as a researcher.
- Part II offers a process to assist you in conceptualizing and framing your research study.
- Part III contains an overview of quantitative and qualitative research approaches, highlights some of the research methods associated with each, and identifies the similarities and differences between quantitative and qualitative research approaches.
- Part IV is designed to assist you in becoming familiar with data sources for research, contents of a research proposal and a research report, and answers to procedural questions that we are frequently asked.

Exercises are at the end of Parts I and II. Completing the exercises add to your applied understanding of the concepts presented.

We deliberately avoided being highly technical. We want the book to be reader friendly. Our intention is to provide you with rudimentary information about conducting scholarly research. In doing so, you will have the foundation and framework you need to analyze, apply, synthesize, and evaluate resources and the actions you take in your research study, as well as transition to research materials that are more detailed.

So, take a deep breath. Let it out slowly and let us start unraveling the mysteries of research.

Cynthia L. Jackson
St. Croix, VI
George R. Taylor
Temple Hills, MD
2007

RESEARCH PRELIMINARIES

Often novice researchers proceed with conducting a research study without acknowledging and considering important details requiring reflection and understanding prior to actually conducting the rescarch study. In Part I we discuss the preliminary essentials associated with undertaking scholarly research.

CHAPTER 1

WHAT IS SCHOLARLY RESEARCH?
WHAT MAKES A RESEARCHER?

By nature humans are curious. They want to know answers to questions or test their observations and ideas about the world in which they live. Almost everyday people do research to solve a problem or answer a question. Courtney wants to know the telephone number of the closest paint store. Kendall wants to know why the fan comes on by itself. While these examples are illustrations of research at its simplest level they demonstrate that doing research is a familiar experience. With the introduction of personal computers and Internet in offices, homes, and schools conducting everyday research has become readily accessible, and now perhaps, second nature.

Yes, research is a familiar experience, but for many, scholarly research is unfamiliar. In this book, we are concerned with scholarly research.

WHAT IS SCHOLARY RESEARCH?

Scholarly research is an investigation or inquiry of a topic based on the generation of data. Data are generated to answer questions or test hypotheses. In this way, research study outcomes become building blocks of knowledge.

Research requires a systematic approach. The approach is known as the research process. There is logic to the manner in which you, the researcher, undertake and conduct an investigation. A reasonable plan is exhibited in all scholarly research

Research is unbiased. While what is studied is based on your bias due to your particular interests, the process used to answer research questions, or test hypotheses, is to be free of your personal, preconceived notions of what should be the outcomes of your study. The data you gather are to be verifiable and impartially interpreted.

Gay and Airasian (2003), Lang and Heiss (1998), and Leedy and Ormrod (2004) provide descriptions of the characteristics of research. Incorporating their work with our experiences, we identify nine attributes of research. Taken as a whole, the attributes represent the research process. In this book, we address the first five attributes, which encompass conceptualizing and framing a research study.

Attribute 1

Research ideas begin with personal observations of the researcher. The actions, events or phenomenon that you observe in your environment and read about spark your curiosity, wondering, or speculation about something. Your questioning, based on your personal observations, begins the research process.

Attribute 2

Research occurs in the context of issues or concerns in a field of study or discipline. In all fields of study and disciplines there are debates occurring on certain topics. In the field of Education, one debate topic is about school choice. A debate topic occurring in the discipline of Psychology is assessment and referral practices. Through your readings about the topic, certain themes or issues begin to emerge that are consistent or inconsistent with what you have observed. It is through reflection on the emerging issues from your observations and readings that you begin to develop inquisitiveness about an element of the topic you want to investigate.

Attribute 3

Research topics are problems or concerns that are identified by the researcher. The identified problem for your study is a personal decision based on your passion about the topic or particular interest. The identified problem evokes questions of "Who is . . . ?", "What causes . . . ?", "When does . . . ?", "Where can . . . ?", or "Why do . . . ?" You determine what problem in the broader topic of interest you will study. For example, if the topic is school choice, you might decide that the aspect of school choice to study will be the use of vouchers, or it could be equity and equality considerations, or perhaps, benefits to students and or teachers. The final aspect of school choice that is studied is your decision. That decision is based on your personal interest in the topic.

Attribute 4

Research requires a clear and unambiguous stated problem. Your overarching, unresolved focus of interest is the research problem. When you are clear about the problem you will investigate, it is possible to state it in one precise, grammatically correct sentence. This sentence is called the research sentence. The research sentence has to be stated clearly from the beginning. A clear research sentence enables you to determine what is appropriate for your research study and what is not appropriate for your research study. Returning to the topic of school choice as a research topic, you might decide to investigate the benefits of school choice for teachers.

4

Having made a decision on the research topic, you must now determine what benefits will be examined. There are several components associated with the benefits of school choice for teachers. The components include, but are not limited to, shared-values with families, academic freedom, and control of educational operations. You decide what component of the benefits of school choice for teachers will be investigated and then develop the specific component into a research sentence. For example, you decided to study the nature of shared educational values between teachers and parents whose children participate in school choice programs. A possible research sentence is, "The purpose of the study is to describe the influence of shared educational values of teachers and parents participating in school choice programs on educational outcomes." Another possible research sentence is, "The purpose of the study is to determine if there is a relationship between the shared educational values of teachers and parents participating in school choice programs and educational outcomes."

Attribute 5

Research problems are address by asking and obtaining answers to research questions, or by posing and testing hypotheses. Research questions or hypotheses are the subcomponents of the research problem. When the research questions are answered or the hypotheses tested, the results provide you with an understanding of the research problem you posed in the research sentence. After developing the research sentence, the next step is to analyze the research problem for its appropriate subcomponents - research questions or hypotheses.

Two possible research questions for the first research sentence example under Attribute 4 could be, "What are the educational values of teachers involved in school choice programs concerning education?" "What are the educational values of parents of children involved in school choice programs concerning education?"

Two possible hypotheses for the second research sentence in Attribute 4 above are, "Teachers who share the same educational values as the parents of children in school choice programs will have fewer classroom management problems than teachers who do not share the same educational values of parents." "When teachers and parents of children in school choice programs share the same educational values, parents' participation in school is higher than when the values are not shared."

Research becomes cumbersome and unmanageable when the research questions or hypotheses are not clearly identified. Answers to the research questions or test results of hypotheses are the resolution of the research problem.

Attribute 6

Research momentum is maintained through the research questions or hypotheses. Research questions or hypotheses determine the literature that needs to be reviewed, whether the research is primarily quantitative or qualitative, the data that will be needed, and the research methods to use. The research questions or hypotheses are the bases for analyzing the data gathered, and stating the findings from the data. Conclusions and interpretations made are based on the findings to answer research questions and the tested hypotheses.

Attribute 7

Research has to be planned. Research is not an aimless and undirected activity. You are not merely looking something up and engaging in activities in "hope" that answers might be found. You engage in purposeful, goal-directed activities that are established through conscious planning. The nature of the research plan is determined by the content of the research sentence, generally, and the research questions or hypotheses, specifically.

The research plan details who will be involved in the research study, data needed to answer the research questions or test the hypotheses, when the study will begin and end, where the research study will occur, why the research study is being conducted, and how the study will be conducted. The research plan is clear enough for others to understand your rationale for engaging in activities to conduct the research as well as to be able to replicate your study.

Attribute 8

Research is concerned with making meaning of data. Data are facts, events, and observations that have the potential of being meaningful to answer the research questions or test hypotheses. Data are gathered and analyzed in relation to the research questions or hypotheses. The importance of the data is based on the meaning you give them. The meaning given the data is bound by the study's research sentence, and research questions or hypotheses first posed.

Attribute 9

Research is shared with others. Scholarly research requires not only answering questions you might have or testing your hypotheses of observations and ideas, it requires sharing what is found with others and holding it up to scrutiny. Research on a particular problem should not end with one study. The results of your study should provoke thought, dialogue and additional research on the problem. These occur as a result of sharing your research with others. Research becomes scholarship when it is shared with other scholars as well as larger communities who could be interested and or benefit from your study. For graduate learners, the first audience of scholars is usually the doctoral or master's committee. Research can also become scholarship when it is shared at professional conferences, published, or addressed in other public forums designed for dialogue and inquiry.

Sharing research is what gives research its cyclical quality. Ultimately, the end product of one research study should generate new research studies.

WHAT MAKES A RESEARCHER?

Who is in control of the unbiased, systematic investigation or inquiry? YOU! You determine what will be investigated, how it will be investigated, and give meaning to the data gathered to address your research questions or hypotheses. More specifically, you determine the purpose of the study and research questions or hypotheses, develop the research design, interpret the data, make conclusions and suggest appropriate subsequent studies. Conducting all these tasks makes you a researcher.

Gathering the data, such as conducting interviews, administering questionnaires or applying a treatment, does not have to be done by the researcher. Corporations, where research is conducted, and large universities often hire people to perform those tasks. They are usually called research assistants or research associates. The researcher has developed or identified the instruments or treatments that will be used. The researcher has determined how the instruments will be used or treatments applied. But it is not required that the researcher administers the instruments or treatments.

Researchers determine the methodology that will be used. But, the intricacy and difficulty of the research methodology does not make you a researcher. The appropriate methodology or methodologies used in a research study are determined by the nature of the research questions or hypotheses, and to some extent by the number of research participants in the study. Therefore, the level of sophistication and complexity of the methodology or methodologies is determined, generally, by the research sentence, and specifically, by the research questions or hypotheses.

In summary, the researcher conceptualizes and frames the study, designs a research plan and makes meaning of data.

CHAPTER 2

COMMUNICATION AND RESEARCH

As noted in Chapter 1, research becomes scholarship when it is shared with audiences of other researchers and those who are interested in the research topic. Sharing research is a form of communication. Therefore, your ability to communicate is critical. Your ideas must be presented with clarity and the language must be precise.

KEEPING YOUR VOICE

First and foremost, it is important that you keep in mind that one writes research to communicate with a reader who does not have access to the researcher. Research is written for the reader, and *not* the researcher.

Thinking clearly and being able to articulate what you are thinking is the beginning of the research process. Unclear writing is a sign of unclear thinking.

As a researcher, you are concerned with establishing a logical argument for studying the stated research problem, and reaching the conclusions and interpretations that you make. How well your argument is accepted by others is in large part based on how well you communicate with readers.

Remember, you should be able to state your research problem in one, grammatically correct sentence. Based on this one sentence you determine the research questions or hypotheses, the literature you need to review, the data you need to gather, the research conclusions you draw, and the interpretations that you make.

For many novice researchers writing the research proposal or report, such as a thesis or dissertation, is approached with trepidation. Often novice researchers begin the writing process using words that they believe will impress the reader but are not part of their vocabulary. Frequently the "impressive words" are used incorrectly. We presume that if you have reached the level of graduate education then you have the needed vocabulary to be articulate about your research study. Therefore, keep your voice and vocabulary, but use it with precision.

Use the first definition of the word in the dictionary. For example, a word that is over used and misused is "impact." The first definition of the word "impact" is, to strike with force. Suppose you titled a research report "The Impact of Testing on Third Grade Children." Based on the title and the first definition of "impact" the title means that the children are hit with the tests. More appropriate substitutes for "impact" could be "influence," "pressure," "effect," "affect," " power," "control," "repercussions," or "emphasis." The appropriate substitute will depend on the exact meaning you want to convey.

Writing mechanics for literature and research are the same. Sentences present one idea. Paragraphs are the explanation of one idea through a series of sentences. There has to be a topic sentence in a paragraph, with additional sentences providing specific related information to the topic sentence. Subject-verb agreement is a requirement.

In 9th grade English composition, Ms. Hohum always said to vary the words in a composition to make the reading interesting and entertaining. Research is not written for entertainment. It is crucial not to vary the essential words in a research study. Key terms and variables will have to be defined in a research proposal and report. They are defined because they have specific meanings in your study. Consistently use the same terms throughout the study. If the term "sheriff" is used, do not substitute it for other terms such as "peace officer" or "police" when writing. Changing terms can lead the reader to think that you are writing about something else, but have not explained or defined it.

In research it is more important to use facts rather than opinions. Opinions cannot achieve the same force as actual facts. However, there are times when no evidence exists, except for expert opinions. When an expert's opinion is quoted, you should introduce it with a phase such as "In Moite's opinion . . . " The reader should be informed that the statement given is an opinion and not a statement of fact based on research.

Get to the point! Sometimes novice researcher waste too much time and space writing useless remarks that never seem to arrive at a main issue or have anything to do with the study. Not only do you want to be selective with the words you use, of equal importance you need to be selective with the comments and ideas included in a research proposal and report. State the point you are making directly. Refrain from adding comments and descriptions that have little or nothing to do with your study.

In everyday personal and professional communications there is a tendency to speak and write in a type of shorthand. Colloquialisms, professional jargon and acronyms are used knowing that the person to whom the communication is directed will understand. The increased use of email seems to exacerbate the use of shorthand.

As a researcher, you cannot make the same assumption about with whom you will communicate. You will identify the specific audiences for whom you are writing, but there might be unknown audiences. Even with identified audiences, professional jargon and acronyms can vary. For example, in a research study you identify social workers as one audience. However, the professional jargon and acronyms for the same type of program or process can vary from state to state and even agency to agency. In addition, police might find your study useful but has no knowledge of the professional jargon and acronyms that are used in social service agencies.

Words with dual meaning, ambiguous language, and judgmental language are to be avoided in research. An example of each concern follows:

- *Dual meaning* – A word can have more than one meaning depending on the context in which it is used. Each italicized word can be substituted with a more precise word:
  Example A. She wanted to get her computer *fixed*.
  Example B. The bank *fixed* the problem with the check.
  In Example A, *fixed* means repaired. In Example B, *fixed* means corrected.

- *Ambiguous Language* – Similar to dual meaning is the concern that the language used is clear and precise. Frequently, the lack of clarity is because terms are relative. What has one meaning for one person often has a different meaning for another person. Review the two examples below. The first sentence is ambiguous. The second sentence is a precise writing of what is meant.
  Example A. He was driving fast. (ambiguous)
  He was driving 45 in a 25 mile an hour speed zone. (precise)
  Example B. The elderly population is increasing. (ambiguous)
  The population 60 and older has increased by 20% since 2001. (precise)

- *Judgmental Language* – In an attempt to defend your point of view sometimes you might use laudatory or derogatory terms in association with a concept. In research writing you are to be unbiased. As mentioned earlier, as humans it is not possible to be totally unbiased. As the researcher, the topic you choose, and how it is conceptualized and framed are forms of bias. This type of bias depends on your specific interest in a topic. But, when writing research the language used should be neutral. The words in *italic* are examples of judgmental language.
  Example A. The legislator *wielded her power* to have her bill passed. (judgmental)
  The legislator used her relationships with other legislators and some policymakers to have the bill passed. (neutral)
  Example B. *Looking tired*, he stated with *fierce determination* that he would complete his doctoral program. (judgmental)
  He stated, "I will complete my doctoral program." (neutral)

FORM AND STYLE MANUALS

There is nothing exciting, entertaining or intellectually stimulating about form and style manuals. Their content is not something you memorize. However, manuals are important reference tools for communicating in scholarly works. Form and style manuals provide the necessary guidelines for uniformity in writing research.

Form and style refers to two communication concerns. Form is the manner in which the research proposal or report is organized or arranged. Style has to do with writing mechanics and the way ideas are expressed and substantiated.

Three form and style manuals are most prevalently used in scholarly writing. The *Publication Manual of the American Psychological Association (APA)* is used not only by psychologist, but it is the most frequently used form and style manual for education and several of the social sciences fields of study and disciplines. (Because the authors are in education and psychology, the APA form and style are used in the *Primer.*) *Chicago Manual of Style* is used in the social sciences, the sciences and mathematics, and sometimes education. Researchers in language and literature use the *Modern Language Association (MLA) Style Manual*.

The information in form and style manuals changes over time. The introduction of electronic information in research proposals and reports created the most recent changes. Therefore, it is important to be sure that you are using the most current edition of the form and style manual.

Generally, the content of form and style manuals is for submitting manuscripts for publication to organizations that developed the manuals. Educational institutions, professional associations, governmental agencies and publishers also use form and style manuals. Which form and style manual is used is contingent on the form and style policies of the organization. Unless the form and style manual is developed for a specific field of study or discipline it is highly likely that the four types of organizations will have caveats to the form and style manual it requires.

Sometimes, but rarely, an organization will let the writer decide on the form and style manual that will be used. In this case, you should select a form and style manual that is consistent with what is used most frequently in your field of study, or discipline, or the focus of the organization. For example, if you were writing a report for the United States Department of Education, the *MLA Style Manual* would not be appropriate.

Regardless of the form and style manual used, they all focus on the same specific concerns, but will require different ways to address them. Appropriately following the style and form manual provides uniformity and consistency in the communication process of research.

Some of the common types of forms and style manual concerns addressed are highlighted below. Often the concerns are not mutually exclusive. In other words, many of the concerns are not limited to form or style. The concerns be-

low are by no means an exhaustive list of the types of concerns in a form and
style manual.

- Abbreviations and Acronyms – Typically, abbreviations and acronyms
  are not used in scholarly writing. Those that are acceptable are ones that
  are known within a field of study or discipline. When they are acceptable and how they are to be written are explained.
- Appendices – Appendices are the collection of all materials too lengthy
  to be included in the body of the text, because they interfere with the
  flow of reading the text, or they are supplemental materials for understanding the study. Form and style manuals explain the expectations for
  what is appropriate for appendices, the format of appendences and the
  order of appendices.
- Bibliographic and Reference List Entries – A bibliography is an extensive list of materials you read related to the research topic. A
  bibliography includes all of the materials cited in the research proposal
  or report. In addition, a bibliography includes materials not cited in the
  research proposal or report, but contributed to informing your understanding about and knowledge of the research topic. Bibliographies are
  usually used in extensive research reports such as theses, dissertations
  and grant reports. A reference list has only the materials cited in the research proposal or report. Reference lists tend to be used primarily in
  research proposals, journal articles and term papers. The purpose of bibliographies and reference lists is to enable the reader to locate the
  materials you used. A form and style manual provides guidelines for entries in these lists. The guidelines include the format for and order of
  listing the materials, and the information required for each entry, depending on the resource type.
- Citations in the Text and Footnotes – Citations and footnotes are the ac-
  knowledgement of the ideas or concepts of others included in your
  research proposal or report. Citations and footnotes avoid the notion of
  plagiarism. All citations and footnotes in the text or body of the research
  proposal or report are to be included in the bibliography or reference
  list. When citation and footnotes are needed and how they are written
  are explained.
- Headings – Key to assisting the reader in reading a research proposal or
  report is the use of headings. Headings divide the information in the research proposal or report into sections that need to be highlighted.
  Headings can be used to highlight a new section of a proposal or report.
  For example, in a book or dissertation you would have chapter titles.
  Headings are also used as a means of transition within the text or body
  of the research proposal or report. The appropriate use of headings and
  how they are written, are explained in a form and style manual.

- Manuscript Preparation – Overall, the purpose of form and style manuals is to explain how to prepare a manuscript for presentation to others. In form and style manuals when manuscript preparation is discussed, the focus is on the mechanics of the physical appearance of a manuscript. The mechanics include margins, page, numbering, font style and size, paper size and weight, and spacing to name a few.
- Numbers – Few research proposals or reports are written without the use of numbers. When you review a form and style manual it becomes clear that all numbers are not written the same way. The writing of numbers depends on the value and nature of the number. Form and style manuals contain the guidelines for writing numbers.
- Quotations – When using the exact words of another in your research proposal or report, quotations are used. When a quotation is appropriate, the acceptable length of quotations and how to include quotations are explained.
- Tables and Figures – Tables and figures are used in research proposals or reports to draw a picture of data or general information. Sometimes, a picture can explain the data or information better than just words alone. Form and style manuals have instructions on how to develop the table or figure, the format for them and when they should be used.
- Writing Mechanics – A section reviewing basic writing mechanics, such as the use of punctuations, grammar, sentence structure, and paragraphing is included in manuals.
- Bias Language – Form and style manuals have a section on how to avoid bias language. Bias language is discriminatory words and phrases that portray negative images and attitudes about others because of their race or ethnicity, gender, sexual orientation, religion, age or disability.

Keep in mind that a form and style manual is a reference tool. As a tool it is to be used for the purpose of applying its content to aid in communicating with a reader. Determine the form and style manual that is most appropriate and use it consistently.

CHAPTER 3

LITERATURE AND RESEARCH

Literature is a critical component of research. Primarily, literature is books and journal articles; however, literature can include printed resources such as government documents, technical reports, professional conference proceedings and papers, and reports form private organizations to name a few.

Increasingly, but cautiously, information from websites, electronic databases and online journals are used. You should be selective about the websites, and electronic online sources that your use. Be sure that information obtained from the Internet is from reputable sources. Governmental websites and databases, information from professional associations, and university online journals are considered reputable Internet sources for research.

In this chapter the use of literature, evaluation of literature, and the categories of literature are discussed. Understanding the nature of the three illustrates the breath and depth of reading that is needed for a research study. In addition, it amplifies the need for a great deal of reading, analysis and evaluation of what is read to produce a scholarly research study and report.

USE OF LITERATURE

Literature serves three purposes for and in a research proposal or report. First, it is used to assist you in conceptualizing and framing your research study. Second, it is included in a section of the research proposal and report, usually titled "Review of Literature." Finally, the literature in your research report is used as the basis to compare and contrast your research findings, and for developing conclusions and interpretations.

Literature to Conceptualize and Frame the Study

Once you have decided on the general research topic, you delve into a board based preliminary reading about the topic. This type of reading enables you to understand the topic, its historical and contemporary aspects, the cross section of views on the topic, and what is known about the topic. It is through this type of reading that you begin to determine your specific focus on the topic, and puts boundaries on what you want to study.

There are several benefits to doing extensive preliminary reading before you determine your specific research topic. Preliminary reading provides you with new ideas about the research topic as well as your research study. It makes it possible for you to identify other research studies with a focus similar to the one you are considering. Through extensive reading you begin to see how the research topic you are considering is related to earlier research on the topic. You also gain insights into what is known about your research topic and what is not known.

Early extensive reading assists you in formulating ideas on the significance of your research and how it will become a building block of knowledge. If the research topic you are considering has been studied before, then you are able to evaluate the uniqueness of your focus on the research topic.

Extensive preliminary reading can enable you to avoid research design and planning errors. Through your reading, you become aware of how other researchers handled research topics similar to the one you are considering. By reading the work of other researchers on the topic, you will be able to identify research approaches and methodologies that have been used. For topics where there is little prior research, you are able to see how other researchers addressed the challenge. Reading is a way to disclose sources of data that you might not have known existed.

Reading is a means to introduce you to significant researchers and research studies related to your research topic. In all likelihood, your research on a topic will not be the first time the specific topic or one related to the topic has been examined. There will be other researchers who have conducted the same or similar research on the topic. Knowing the names of these individuals as well as their studies is essential. Through extensive preliminary reading key researchers on a topic are identified because their names will repeatedly appear in bibliographies and reference lists, and their work will be repeatedly cited. When the names of individuals occur frequently, you should make note of them. These researchers' works might be the foundation on which your research study will become a building block of knowledge. References to these researchers and their research would be expected to be mentioned in the research proposal and report of the study.

In the preliminary reading phase, it is helpful if you develop an annotated bibliography. An annotated bibliography is more than a listing of readings. Although each annotated bibliographic entry includes information for use in a bibliography, the purpose of an annotated bibliography is your summary and evaluation of contents of literature you read. The summary is an explanation of what the literature is about. The evaluation is your critique of the material in relation to its relevance to your research topic, the accuracy of the information compared to similar information, and the objectivity of the authors. The information is written according to the form and style manual you are using. Completing the annotated bibliography enables you to locate the literature should you need to refer to it repeatedly, and saves time for organizing bibliographic information.

Review of Literature

All research proposals and reports include a review of literature. The review of literature for a thesis, dissertation and grant proposals is usually preliminary. It gives the reader an orientation to the nature and scope of material you will include in the final report. The review of literature for a research report, e.g., thesis or dissertation is broader and more in-depth than for the proposal. The review of literature section puts the research study in context to prior research on the topic. While websites and other electronic information can be used in the review of literature, it is expected that the majority of the materials used are from print sources.

The review of literature chapter is not a restatement of the literature. The review of literature is a critical, comprehensive review of related research and information about your research topic. The literature review is to be analytical, and not merely a retelling or listing of the cited studies or information. Through the review of literature, three concerns are addressed: 1) evidence that your study is needed, 2) evidence that the methodology you use is most appropriate for your research questions or hypotheses; and 3) documentation of prior research on your research topic or related research topics.

You provide the literature and research studies that substantiate your point of view on the research topic. But of equal importance, you include literature and research studies that do not substantiate your point of view. In short, both sides of the research argument are presented. For example, you are conducting a research study on black students and standardized tests. You would be expected to discuss the bell curve research in your review of literature for two reasons. First, it is expected for you to be familiar and demonstrate your familiarity with the bell curve research given the nature of the research topic. Second, if you do not agree with the conclusions of bell curve research, you are able to counter the bell curve research results and interpretations with other research on black students and standardized test. (As a reminder, bell curve research concludes that blacks do poorly on standardized test because blacks are inherently not as intelligent as whites.) How you counter the bell curve research, for example, is based on your knowledge and reasoning about the research on the topic.

Literature and research studies are cited in your review of literature chapter, and included in the bibliography or reference list according to the form and style manual that you are using. Studies and information are not just presented as listings of one study or information after another, with each being a paragraph. Compare, analyze, synthesize, and evaluate the various studies and information, while always being sure to demonstrate the relation of the cited studies and information to your research problem and your research questions or hypotheses.

Sufficient information is presented regarding research studies cited in your review of literature. The information includes the purpose of the research study, the general design of the study, the design limitations, and the research study outcomes. Your evaluation of the strengths and weaknesses of the cited research studies in relation to your research problem, and research questions and hypotheses is critical. *Synthesizing Research: A Guide for Literature Reviews* (Cooper, 2001) and *Writing Literature Reviews* (Galvan, 2004) are two books that can assist you in developing your review of literature section.

Literature as a Point of Comparison

The literature in the review of literature is a point of reference to discuss and interpret the findings of your research study. The studies and literature included in your review of literature serve as the basis for comparing and contrasting the findings of your research study.

Comparing and contrasting your study's findings to the literature in the review of literature is done at the end of the study. You determine if and how your research study findings relate to what is known about the research study topic. The "known" is based on what is in your review of literature. Comparing and contrasting makes it possible for you to determine the building block of knowledge of your study.

EVALUATION OF LITERATURE

Never presume that all published research meets the standards for research. It is vital for you to evaluate or judge each piece of literature you review.

Standards of research are the substance and content expected in a research report. It seems fair to say that the standards of research were written for a perfect world. Even good research will fall short of some standards or be flawed. That is part of the manifestation of humans conducting research. However, good research should meet the majority of the standards.

Several of the standards of research are embedded in the attributes of research discussed in Chapter 1. There are criteria of standards of research to evaluate literature. In addition, there are criteria for standards of research to evaluate research literature depending of the type of research methodology used, such as narrative studies, historical studies, or correlation studies.

Gay and Airasian (2003), Girden (2001) and Pyrczak (2003) provide guidelines to evaluate scholarly literature. The following highlights some of their and our general criteria to evaluate research literature you review.

- The Problem - The research problem is stated clearly early in the literature. Included are the issues or background information about the research problem. Providing the issues or background information demonstrates the building block of knowledge and significance of the problem that is studied. Variables and terms related to the research problem are defined.

- Review of Literature – The review of literature relates to the stated research problem. The majority of the cited materials are primary sources. The review of literature is not a restatement or summary of what the authors read. The reviewed literature is compared, analyzed, synthesized and evaluated. Sufficient information is given about all studies that are cited. The authors explain the relation between cited materials and the research problem studied.

- Research Questions or Hypotheses – Specific research questions or hypotheses are stated. Research questions are to be answerable and hypotheses are to be testable. There should be an obvious connection between the research questions or hypotheses and the stated research problem.

- Methods – Research methods are explained in enough detail to demonstrate the logic of the research plan design and methods to be employed to permit a replication of the study. Criteria and procedures to select research participants are clearly described including the rationale, number and characteristics of the research participants. All instruments or treatments are described in terms of reason for selection of the instrument or treatment, what the instruments are to measure, the purpose of the treatment, the validity and or reliability of instruments chosen, and how instruments and treatments are administered. The research design or plan is explained, including sufficient information on how data were gathered and analyzed. Research design, instruments and or treatments, data gathering procedures and analysis limitations are discussed. Human subject protection procedures are addressed.

- Findings – Each research question is answered or each hypothesis is tested. The findings are understandable statements of the results of data analysis.

- Discussion, Conclusions, and Recommendations – A discussion of each finding in relation to the research questions or hypotheses were given. The findings are compared and contrasted to the information in the study's review of literature. Theoretical and practical implications of the findings are discussed. Recommendations are made for further study of the research topic.

PERSPECTIVES ON LITERATURE

Literature being considered for use in a research study needs to be thought about from three perspectives. The first perspective is concerned with the date of the study or information being reviewed. The second perspective is your degree of contact with the original study or information being reviewed. The third perspective is concerned with the original intended audience.

Literature Age

Literature can be divided into two age categories – contemporary and classic. In education and the social science fields of study and disciplines contemporary literature is information that is not more than five or seven years old, respectively. The social science disciplines include: Anthropology, Economics, Political Science, Psychology and Sociology. The reasoning for the five-year or seven-year rule is that knowledge is constantly being generated and new knowledge changes the perspectives of old knowledge. Five or seven years are considered a reasonable length of time for knowledge to be considered "new" or contemporary. The majority of the literature in your review of literature chapter will be contemporary.

If contemporary literature is five or seven years or less then would it not be reasonable to say that all literature that is more that seven years could be called "old" literature? The answer is, "Yes." But all old literature is not classic literature. Pertinent studies are included regardless of how old they are. Classic literature is the foundation on which the knowledge of your research topic is based. Put another way, classic literature is the writings and research that anyone conducting research on your topic is expected to know and cite. For example, if your research topic is grounded in organizational behavior, then citing information from Douglas McGregor's *The Human Side of Enterprise* published 1960 is appropriate. If the research study focuses on the education of African Americans, it would be appropriate to cite Carter G. Woodson's work titled *The Miseducation of the Negro* that was published in 1933.

There will only be a few classics cited in the review of literature. Classics are identified through extensive preliminary reading and dialogues with others who have conducted studies on or are knowledgeable about the topic or related topics.

Degree of Original Contact

The degree of original contact concerns if you are reading the original study or another author's interpretation of a study or information. If the original study or information is being reviewed, then you are using primary literature sources. If the study or information is contained in the writing of someone else, then you are reviewing secondary literature sources.

In education and social science research, the majority of the literature in the review of literature is to be from primary sources rather than secondary sources. We say, "the majority", because sometimes it is not possible to obtain an original source. The source might be out-of-print, or had a limited distribution. Then you might find it necessary to use secondary sources. Secondary sources should be used with caution. It is possible that information is taken out of context. It is also possible that the author who is citing the information has a different interpretation of the meaning of the work than that of the original author.

The cautions for using secondary sources are the strengths for using primary sources. Reviewing primary sources allows you to review the information in its original context. It enables you to draw your conclusions and make interpretations about the information. Thus, it is crucial for you to obtain original work, whenever possible.

Original Intended Audiences

All written material is not appropriate for research. When considering literature for research, literature can be divided into two types – popular and scholarly. Popular materials are written for a wide audience. They are generally written between the 5th and 8th grade reading levels. This is done to make the information accessible to a cross section of people. Popular materials tend to provide some facts, as well as opinions of the authors. Frequently, the materials are laden with some form of subtle or obvious propaganda, or judgmental language. They do not require specific evidence of what is stated. Popular materials include, but are not limited to, newspapers, magazines, and many books on bestseller lists. While popular materials are not included in a bibliography or reference list for a research study, sometimes they are a resource for new information. For example, a study's findings on how immigration patterns influence immigration laws and labor relations are reported in a newspaper, you need to get the actual study to review. You would not cite the newspaper article as the source. You would cite the study you reviewed.

Scholarly materials have limited audiences. They provide extensive and specialized knowledge for or about a particular discipline or field of study. The information in these materials is considered insightful, weighty, thoughtful and theoretical. The information in scholarly materials is considered building blocks of knowledge. Yet, all information in scholarly materials does not necessarily stand up to scrutiny. You have to evaluate the content of information in scholarly materials, whatever the source.

CHAPTER 4

LIBRARY RESOURCES
AND ELECTRONIC DATABASES

Knowledge of the tools of research is both necessary and beneficial for you and the research being conducted. There is less of an opportunity for error and bias in your study if you possess a broad knowledge base of research tools.

The purpose of this chapter is to provide information to enhance your knowledge and skills in accessing information sources in printed and electronic forms. Most of the necessary tools can be found or accessed in public and school libraries, and many of the electronic sources can be accessed from home if you have the required programs and linkages. Therefore, this chapter is designed to summarize some of the commonly used library tools by researchers. In addition, the library contains an array of article reviews, summaries, and hard copy references for all fields of interest. Further, for foundation information and data, your library becomes your best source of information because housed on the shelves is documentation of what is known, what has been investigated, and the success of or lack of success of these previous investigations (Taylor, 2000).

In Chapter 3, we addressed the importance of the review of the literature. Extensive use of the library and electronic databases are essential to acquire the literature you will review. Much of the content of this chapter is from Taylor's *Integrating Quantitative and Qualitative Methods in Research* (2000).

LIBRARY RESOURCES

Public and school libraries are primary sources of information; however, they can become primary sources of frustration if you are not familiar with the process of using the available resources to locate or retrieve the desired information. Thus, learning to use the public or school library to find information is an important part of any research endeavor. Further, it might be helpful for you to use the following four sequence suggestions in preparation for a research project:

– Review a variety of literatures on a selected topic to determine if sufficient data are present to conduct the study, as well as, determining whether or not you have the necessary human and physical resources to conduct the study.

– Consult a periodical index to locate recent articles on a selected topic. Choose a periodical in your area of interest; choose only the most recent articles. These articles will provide an overview of the most recent advancements in the field.

- Review the cited bibliography from relevant sources. This will provide additional and more in-depth information in order to know the controversies in the field, as well as to take a position on your research topic.
- Review current yearly publications of research in fields of study and disciplines. Also review abstracts in the field of study or discipline being investigated, and dissertation abstracts. These valuable sources may be found at the reference desk in most libraries. Proper use of these sources will save you countless hours in reading about and focusing your research topic.

Dewey Decimal System

Knowledge of the use of this system can also expedite your time in the library. Within each one of the 10 broad categories of the Dewey Decimal System (DD) are 10 divisions, thus totaling 100 subdivision groups.

00–99	General Works (books about books, magazines, newspapers)
100–199	Philosophy and Psychology (human behavior, excludes psychiatry)
200–299	Religion (history, law, mythology)
300–399	Social Sciences (economics, education, occupations)
400–499	Languages and Communication (linguistics, grammar, dictionaries)
500–599	Pure Sciences (botany, chemistry, physics)
600–699	Technology, Applied Sciences (business, farming, medicine, psychiatry)
700–799	Fine Arts and Recreation (music, sports)
800–899	Literature (plays, poetry, speeches)
900–999	History (biography, geography, and travel books)

Library Sources to Consider

In every field and discipline there are specific reference sources that assist you in locating needed information. Three examples of reference sources follow. Some can be obtained online for a fee. At your public or school library their use is free.

- Abstracts provide a brief overview of information that is published. Two types of abstracts are useful in the early phase of a research study. The two types are abstracts of periodicals and *Dissertation Abstracts*. Abstracts of periodicals provide a synopsis of recent publications in a field of study or discipline. On example of these abstracts is *Psychological Abstracts. Dissertation Abstracts* includes the abstracts from dissertations from institutions in the United States.

– Card catalogs are a master key to quick and efficient use of a library. The arrangement of the card catalog is very similar to that of a dictionary or telephone directory. This alphabetical listing covers a vast array of material including periodicals, encyclopedias, and microfilms which can assist you in locating information relevant to your study.

– Encyclopedias are references that contain alphabetically listed collections of information that range from the general to the specific. In most instances the information is cross-referenced. The reference contains articles written by experts who review and analyze pertinent information for a field or discipline. Three examples of encyclopedias are: *Blackwell Encyclopedia of Political Thought, Encyclopedia of Educational Research*, and *Encyclopedia of Social Work.*

ELECTRONIC DATABASES

Does the word "database", sound technical and forbidding? Does the word make you uncomfortable? It should not because you use databases comfortably every day. In fact, you use them so much, you do not even think about the fact that you are using databases. Typical databases that you might use on any given day include a telephone directory, a dictionary, an encyclopedia, an airline flight guide, or a bibliography. In fact, now that you think about it, you can see that databases have been used to store all kinds of knowledge that you retrieve on a regular basis. A typical database is designed around a central set of facts.

A database is a large organized list of facts and information. A database usually contains text and numbers, but it also can contain still images, sounds, and even video film clips. What is the difference between a list and a database? A database permits you to extract a specific group of facts from a collection of facts. The elaborate paper filing system in your office is a kind of database. However, the databases under discussion here are constructed on computers where pieces of software help people access and retrieve collections of data.

Alphabetical Listing of Electronic Databases

Many public libraries and the majority of academic research libraries subscribe to various electronic databases of use to you. The alphabetical listing below contains information on over 60 commercially available electronic databases related to education and the social sciences.

– *African American Biographical Database (AABD). A general reference most useful for research in education, psychology, and social sciences.* Contains biographic entries on more thousands of famous and everyday African Americans. Biographic entries illuminate on the African

American Experience. Enables access to collection of African American reference works. Entries chronically the Experience beginning with 1790. Database constantly expanding. Published by ProQuest Information and Learning Company. Membership fee.

- *AGRICOLA. A database most useful for research in physical sciences, technology, health sciences, life sciences, social sciences, and sociology.* The database includes more than three million citations, not only on agricultural topics such as agricultural engineering and marketing, animal breeding, entomology, environmental pollution, farm management, foods and feeds, pesticides, veterinary medicine and water resources, but also chemistry, energy geography, human nutrition, life sciences, natural resources and rural sociology. It indexes journal articles, audiovisual materials, book chapters, computer databases, conference proceedings, maps, manuscripts, monographs, serials, software, sound recordings, and technical reports. Starting with 1970. New records added monthly. Published by the National Agriculture Library. Part of the FirstSearch collection of databases.

- *AIDS and Cancer Research. A database most useful for research in health sciences, physical sciences, technology and social sciences.* Index of cancer and AIDS research gathered from worldwide scientific literature summarized in Virology & AIDS Abstracts, Oncogenes & Growth Factors Abstracts, and Immunology Abstracts. The database covers the current year plus the five preceding years. Updated monthly. Published by Cambridge Scientific Abstracts. Part of the FirstSearch collection of databases.

- *America: History and Life. A database most useful for research in humanities and social sciences.* Bibliographic citations and abstracts on research articles from more than 2,100 international journals studying United States and Canadian history from prehistoric times to the present. Includes citations for dissertations, book, film, and video reviews. Beginning with 1982. See: *Historical Abstracts,* for research literature on the history of other countries.

- *American-Indian Multimedia Encyclopedia. A full-text database most useful for research in humanities and social sciences.* Hypertext-linked information on American Indian tribe histories, folklore and religions. Includes biographies. More than 300 full-text documents such as treaties and relevant legislation, glossaries, timetables, and a directory of relevant United States and Canadian museums and societies. Includes color videos, sound files, illustrations, maps, and historical photographs. Keyword and Boolean searching of text and multimedia files.

- *ArticleFirst. A general reference most useful for research in arts, humanities, business, economics, statistics, education, psychology, physical sciences, technology, health sciences and social sciences.* Bibliographic citations describe items listed on the table of contents pages of more than 13,000 journals in science, technology, medicine, social science, business, the humanities and popular culture. Starting with 1990. Updated daily. Published by OCLC. Part of the FirstSearch collection of databases.

- *Basic BIOSIS. A database most useful for research in life sciences, physical sciences, technology and social sciences* More than 300,000 records from 350 of the basic core of life science journals found in college and university libraries beginning 1994. Provides information on developments in 96 subject areas of the biological and biomedical sciences covering the most prestigious journals. Updated monthly. Formerly known as BIOSIS/FS. A subset, by journal title and year, of BIOSIS Previews. Published by BIOSIS. Part of the FirstSearch collection of databases.

- *Biography Index. A general reference most useful for research in the arts, humanities, business, economics, statistics, education, psychology, current events, and social sciences.* Biographical index to more than 2,700 English-language periodicals plus biographical materials in 1,800 books. Includes autobiographies, bibliographies, individual and collective biographies, critical studies, fiction, drama, pictorial works, poetry, juvenile literature, obituaries, journals, collections of letters, book reviews and interviews. More than 1,800 books added each year. Data begins July 1984. Updated monthly. Published by H.W. Wilson Company. Part of the FirstSearch collection of databases.

- *Book Review Digest. A general reference most useful for research in arts, humanities, education, psychology, social sciences and current events.* Index with abstracts to book reviews appearing in some 100 periodicals in the United States, Canada, and Great Britain, covering more than 7,000 adult and children's books each year. Includes English-language fiction and nonfiction. Concise critical evaluations from 95 selected journals in the humanities, sciences, and social sciences, as well as library review media. Entries begin January 1983. Updated monthly. Published by H.W. Wilson Company. Part of the FirstSearch collection of databases.

- *Books In Print. A general reference most useful for research in humanities, life sciences, technology, social sciences, and current events.* Information on 2,000,000 in-print, out-of-print and forthcoming books from more than 44,000 North American publishers. Publisher-verified information on all United States books in print. Includes more than 900,000 new or revised records each year. Covers scholarly, technical, popular, adult, juvenile, and reprint titles. Publisher information. Updated weekly. Published by Reed Reference Publishing. Part of the FirstSearch collection of databases.

- *CARL UnCover. A general-reference full-text database most useful for research in the arts, humanities, business, economics, statistics, educa-*

tion, psychology, and social sciences. Provides access to contents of 17,000 current English-language journals. More than 7,000,000 articles are available with 5,000 being added daily. UnCover addresses virtually all fields of study. This commercial document delivery service provides free table of contents information for each journal. If an article was published with an abstract, UnCover provides the abstract. Search the database by subject or name, or view the contents of particular issues after choosing a journal title. While there is no fee for using the UnCover search capabilities, there are fees for articles ordered through the service.

- *Census/Population-Housing 2000. A database most useful for research in business, economics, statistics and social sciences.* See United States Census of Population and Housing, 2000.
- *Chicano Database. A general reference most useful for research in education, psychology, social sciences, and current events.* Chicano Database (CDB) contains more than 42,000 bibliographic citations describing the Mexican-American (Chicano) experience. Also, describes the broader Latino experience including Puerto Ricans, Cuban Americans, and Central American immigrants. Reference books, Chicano journals, mainstream journals, anthologies and other forms. A comprehensive bibliographic resource for information about Chicano or Mexican-American topics. Data entries begin with 1992. Published in English and Spanish by Chicano Studies Library University of California, Berkeley.
- *CIA World FactBook. A general reference full-text database most useful for research in economics, social sciences, statistics, technology and current events.* Electronic version of the FactBook printed annually by the Central Intelligence Agency for United States Government officials. Information provided by the American Geophysical Union, Bureau of the Census, Central Intelligence Agency, Defense Intelligence Agency, Defense Mapping Agency, Defense Nuclear Agency, Department of State, Foreign Broadcast Information Service, Maritime Administration, National Science Foundation Polar Information Program, naval Maritime Intelligence Center, Office of Territorial and International Affairs, United States Board on Geographic Names, United States Coast Guard, and others.
- *Code of Federal Regulations (CFR). A full-text database most useful for research in arts, business, economics, education, government regulation, health sciences, humanities, life sciences, physical sciences, psychology, social sciences, statistics, technology and current event.* CFR database contains rules and regulations established by the executive departments and agencies of the federal government divided into 50 Titles representing broad areas subject to federal regulation. Once a regulation appearing in the Federal Register becomes effective, it is

published in the Code of Federal Regulations. CD-ROM updated monthly.

- *Consumers Index. A full-text database most useful for research in social sciences, business, economics and statistics.* A subject index to the contents of more than 100 periodicals. The database provides information categorized from general (the home) to the specific (automobiles), by periodical (Consumer Reports) or by brand name (Coca-Cola). The information includes consumers, librarians and library users, business professionals, and educational instructors. Some records are linked to full-text articles. Published by The Pierian Press, Inc. Part of the First-Search collection of databases.

- *Contents First (Contents 1st). A general reference most useful for research in education, humanities, social sciences, life sciences, psychology and current events.* Table of contents page and holdings information for 13,000 journals in science, technology, medicine, social science, business, the humanities, and popular culture. Some journals in other languages are included. Data entries begin with January 1990. Updated daily. Published by OCLC. Part of the FirstSearch collection of database.

- *DataTimes EyeQ. A general reference most useful for research in social sciences, business, technology, and current events.* Indexes articles in 100 newspapers from major United States cities and regions including Commerce Business Daily, Investor's Business Daily, and the Christian Science Monitor. International titles include 34 publications from Canada, Europe, Middle East, Asia and Pacific Rim. Articles, reviews, editorials, and commentaries. Entries begin with February 1, 1996. Updated daily. Published by the Data Times Corporation. Part of the FirstSearch collection of databases.

- *Dissertation Abstracts. A general reference useful for research in any field including the arts, business, current events, economics, education, health sciences, humanities, life sciences, psychology, social sciences, statistics, and technology.* Abstracts of dissertations accepted at accredited institutions since 1861. Includes the complete range of academic subjects. Covers every doctoral dissertation completed in the United States at accredited institutions. Includes some master's theses and foreign language dissertations.. Updated monthly. Published by UMI. Part of the FirstSearch collection of databases.

- *Dow Jones News Retrieval Service. A general reference full-text database most useful for research in the arts, humanities, business, economics, statistics, education, psychology, social sciences, and current events.* Dow Jones Publications Library is a resource of more than 6 million documents and more than 3,400 trade and business publications including 48 of the top 50 newspapers. Uses the Publications Information on just about any subject, region, industry, company or person. Trade publication covers everything from farming to pharmaceuticals, to banking, mining and marketing.

- *EBSCO MasterFILE. A general reference full-text database most useful for research in the arts, humanities, business, economics, statistics, education, psychology, social sciences, and current events.* Index to 2,300-plus business, humanities, general science, social science, health, and trade periodicals. The complete text of the articles from many of these periodicals may be available through this database with the earliest coverage, beginning in 1990. Abstracting began in 1984. Updated weekly.

- *Economic Literature (EconLit). A database most useful for research in business, economics, statistics, and social sciences.* Subject indexing and citations with abstracts to articles from more than 400 economics journals, more than 500 collective volumes per year, plus books, dissertations, and working papers. Subject indexing and abstracts of books and subject indexing of dissertation titles are included. Entries begin with January 1969. Updated monthly. Published by American Economic Association. Part of the FirstSearch collection of databases.

- *Education Abstracts. A database most useful for research in education and psychology.* Indexing more than 400 English-language periodicals and yearbooks published in the United States and elsewhere. Subjects include administration, teaching methods and curriculum, literacy, government funding, and more. Updated monthly. Published by H.W. Wilson Company. Part of the FirstSearch collection of databases.

- *eHRAF. A full-text database most useful for research in social sciences.* See: Human Relations Area Files.

- *Encyclopedia Britannica. A general reference full-text database most useful for research in the humanities, social sciences, life sciences, physical sciences, technology, health sciences, and current events.* See: Britannica.

- *Environmental Periodicals Bibliography. A database most useful for research in physical sciences, technology and social sciences.* More than 450,000 bibliographic citations. References include papers and reports on air, water, and land pollution, energy issues, human ecology, and nutrition and health. Entries begin with 1972. Updated twice a year. Published by the Environmental Studies Institute, Santa Barbara, CA.

- *Environmental RouteNet. A full-text database most useful for research in physical sciences, technology, and social sciences.* Bibliographic and full-text sources of interest to environmental science and accessible through 23 environmental subject categories. RouteNet includes daily news highlights, research, statistics, standards, patents, legislation, regulations, site-specific information, publications, information on education, grants and funding, etc.

- *Environmental Sciences and Pollution Management. A database most useful for research in physical sciences, technology, and social sciences.* A database of environmental science, including toxic hazards of chemicals, pharmaceuticals, and other substances; air, marine, and freshwater pollution, as well as biochemical applications in water treatment and pollution. Published by Cambridge Scientific Abstracts. Part of the FirstSearch collection of databases.

- *Educational Resources Information Center (ERIC). A database most useful for research in education, psychology, and social sciences.* More than 800,000 bibliographic references to published and unpublished sources on thousands of educational topics. Includes journal articles, books, theses, curricula, conference papers, and standards and guidelines. Information from *Resources in Education* (RIE) and *Current Index to Journals in Education (CIJE).* Starting with 1966. Updated monthly. Published by United States Department of Education. Part of the FirstSearch collection of databases.

- *EventLine. A database most useful for research in current events, the humanities, business, economics, physical sciences, social sciences, and statistics.* A multidisciplinary, multinational database of past and coming events. Covers all the sciences, industry and business, and major sporting events. Data on conventions, symposia, exhibitions, trade fairs, and major sporting events. Dates and locations of meetings, marketing strategy planning, travel planning assistance, statistics on meetings trends. Published by Elsevier Science Publishing Company. Part of the FirstSearch collection of databases.

- *Expanded Academic Index and Full-Text ASAP. A general reference full-text database most useful for research in the arts, humanities, social sciences, business, economics, statistics, and current events.* See: InfoTrac SearchBank.

- *FactSearch. A general reference full-text database most useful for research in business, economics, the humanities, statistics, social sciences, government information and current events.* A guide to statistical statements on current social, economic, political, environmental, and health issues from 1,000 newspapers, periodicals, newsletters and documents such as *The Christian Science Monitor,* the *Congressional Record*, congressional hearings, daily press briefings of the White House, State Department, and Department of Defense. Some links to free full-text documents. Entries cover 1984 to present. Updated every six weeks. Based on the publication *A Matter of Fact.* Published by The Pierian Press, Inc. Part of the FirstSearch collection of databases.

- *FastDoc. A full-text database most useful for research in the arts, humanities, social sciences, business, economics, and statistics.* The database covers more than 900,000 articles in all disciplines from more than 1,000 journals. Companion to ArticleFirst database. Published by OCLC. Part of the FirstSearch collection of databases.
- *GEOBASE. A database most useful for research in physical sciences, technology, and social sciences.* More than 600,000 abstracts covering worldwide literature of geography, geology, ecology, international development and related disciplines. Subjects include cartography, climatology, energy, environment, geomorphology, hydrology, photogrammetry, sedimentology, geochemistry, geophysics, paleontology, petrology, and volcanology. More than 2,000 journals fully covered and an additional 3,000 selectively covered. Abstracts begin with 1980. Updated monthly. Published by Elsevier Science Publishers. Part of the FirstSearch collection of databases.
- *GPO Access. A full-text database most useful for research in government information.* Index to more than 450,000 records for documents including all types of United States government documents such as the Federal Register, the web version of *The Monthly Catalog*, congressional reports, hearings, debates, and records; judiciary materials; documents issued by executive departments such as Defense, State, Labor, Office of the President, etc. Entries begin July 1976. Updated monthly.
- *GPO Monthly Catalog. A full-text database most useful for research in government information and social sciences.* Index to more than 450,000 United States government documents such as congressional reports, hearings, debates, and records; judiciary materials; executive department documents such as Defense, State, Labor, Office of the President, etc. Entries cover July 1976 to the present. Updated monthly. Published by United States Government Printing Office. Part of the FirstSearch collection of databases.
- *Historical Abstracts. A database most useful for research in the humanities and social sciences.* Bibliographic citations and abstracts of thousands of world history (from c.1450) research journal articles from more than 2,100 international journals in 50 languages, excluding the United States and Canada, covering prehistoric times to the present. Also cites dissertations and book reviews of recently published books. Abstracts are in English. Searchable by subject, author, title and time period. Data entries begin with 1982. Updated three times a year. Published by the American Historical Association. See: *America: History and Life,* for research literature on the history of the United States or Canada.

- *HRAF. A full-text database most useful for research in the social sciences.* See: Human Relations Area Files.

- *Human Relations Area Files (HRAF CD-ROM and eHRAF Internet). A full-text database most useful for research in the social sciences.* Information on a broad range of cultures worldwide, from scholarly books, dissertations, journal articles and conference papers. Disciplines covered include anthropology, geology, history, psychology, medicine, ethnic studies, fine arts, literature, social work, law, and archaeology.

- *H.W. Wilson Select. A full-text database most useful for research in the humanities and social sciences.* Database includes more than 430 periodical titles. All records have companion ASCII full-text. Published by H.W. Wilson Company. Part of the FirstSearch collection of databases.

- *Ideal. A general reference full-text database most useful for research in business, economics, statistics, education, psychology, social sciences, and current events.* International Digital Electronic Access Library. (IDEAL) contains the full-text of all 175 primary research journals from *The Academic Press* beginning with 1996 issues. Articles are in Adobe Acrobat PDF format.

- *Index to Legal Periodicals and Books. A database most useful for research in business, economics, statistics, social sciences and the law.* Article indexing from some 620 legal journals, yearbooks, institutes, bar association organs, law reviews, and government publications originating in the United States, Canada, Great Britain, Ireland, Australia, and New Zealand. Covers all areas of jurisprudence including court decisions, legislation, and original scholarship. Includes book reviews. Covers August 1981 to the present. Updated monthly. Published by H.W. Wilson Company. Part of the FirstSearch collection of databases.

- *InfoTrac SearchBank. A general reference full-text database most useful for research in the arts, humanities, social sciences, business, economics, statistics, physical sciences, technology, and current events.* InfoTrac SearchBank's Expanded Academic Index and Full-Text ASAPincludes full-text articles from more than 500 academic periodicals and indexing and abstracting for nearly 1,600 scholarly and general interest periodicals. Database includes the New York Times, Wall Street Journal, Congressional Quarterly weekly report, Newsweek and the Harvard Business Review. SearchBank's Business & Company ProFile ASAP provides full text business journals and current company data. Indexing and abstracting for approximately 900 business and trade periodicals, and full text for 460 titles. Data entries begin with 1980. Updated daily. Published by Information Access Company.

- *LEXIS-NEXIS. A general reference full-text database most useful for research in the arts, business, economics, education, government information, health sciences, humanities, life sciences, physical sciences, psychology, social sciences, statistics, technology, and current events.* LEXIS offers full-text of legal materials, court cases, state statutes, federal agency materials, and the United States Code. NEXIS news and business information service provides full-text of international, national and regional newspapers, news wires, magazines, trade journals and business publications, including the New York Times and the Des Moines Register. NEXIS has more than 7,100 sources, of which, 3,700 provide their entire publications online.

- *Library Literature. A database most useful for research in computers, education, information science, library science, psychology and social sciences.* More than 220 library and information science periodicals published internationally in the library and information science fields, along with more than 600 books and 600 monographs per year. Entries start with December 1984. Updated monthly. Published by H.W. Wilson Company. Part of the FirstSearch collection of databases.

- *Linguistics and Language Behavior Abstracts (LLBA). A database most useful for research in communication, linguistics, psychology, and the social sciences.* Includes all aspects of linguistics and language including interpersonal behavior and communication and nonverbal communication. Abstracts start with 1967.

- *Maps & Facts. A database most useful for research in business, economics, education, geography, humanities, social sciences, statistics, and current events.* A world atlas with hundreds of detailed maps and a database of statistical information for 227 countries.

- *Matter-of-Fact Database. A general reference full-text database most useful for research in the arts, business, economics, education, environment, health sciences, humanities, life sciences, physical sciences, political science, psychology, social sciences, statistics, technology, and current events.* Contains original quotes from speeches and written works containing statistics on current social, economic, political, health, environmental, and public policy issues. Twenty-five percent of the abstracts are derived from congressional hearings, 15% from the *Congressional Record*, and the remainder from general interest and specialized periodicals, newsletters, and newspapers. Many records contain World Wide Web addresses for access to the full text of the *Congressional Record*, debates of the Canadian House of Commons, and Handsards of the Australian House of Representatives and Senate. Also included are speeches of the President, White House press briefings, State Department daily press briefings and background notes, electronic newsletters of the World Health Organization, and many other national, regional, and international resources. More than 80,000 bibliographic records with more than 12,000 new records added annually. Covering 1984 to the present. Updated quarterly. Published by the Pierian Press, Inc.

– *Mental Measurements Yearbook. A database most useful for research in education and psychology.* MMY describes more than 1,850 standardized educational, personality, vocational aptitude and psychological tests published commercially. Lists authors, publishers, time requirements, score descriptions, intended populations, validity/reliability data and critical reviews. Published by the Buros Bureau of Mental Measurements.

– *MLA International Bibliography. A database most useful for research in the arts, humanities, language studies and social sciences.* The MLA International Bibliography provides easy access to a vast spectrum of subjects, from the prose of Machiavelli to the poetry of Adrienne Rich, from genres to literary forms, from national literatures to regional dialects. Includes the MLA Bibliography Thesaurus. Indexes critical literary and language scholarship on modern language, literature, linguistics, drama and folklore in more than 4,000 journals and serials published worldwide, as well as books, monographs, essay collections, working papers, proceedings, dissertations and bibliographies. Some 500,000 records with 45,000 added annually. Updated quarterly. Covers 1963 to the present. Published by Modern Language Association of America. Part of the FirstSearch collection of databases.

– *National Newspaper Index. A general reference full-text database most useful for research in the social sciences, technology, business, economics, humanities, statistics, and current events.* Bibliographic index of five national newspapers: *The New York Times, Wall Street Journal, Christian Science Monitor, Washington Post* and *Los Angeles Times.* Covers most recent four years. Updated daily. Published by Information Access Company.

– *National Trade Data Bank. A database most useful for research in government information.* NTDB contains United States import and export information including balance of payments; international investment in the United States and United States investment abroad; operations of United States affiliates of foreign companies; national and international labor; economic, demographic, and energy statistics; international price indexes; world agricultural production and commodity status reports; trade projections and barriers; stock price indexes for G-10 countries; currency exchange rates; and United States export manuals. Published by the United States federal government.

– *NetFirst. A general reference full-text database most useful for research in the arts, humanities, business, economics, statistics, education, psychology, social sciences, government information, and current events.* Database contains bibliographic citations, abstracts, summary descriptions, subject headings, and classification codes for Internet resources including World Wide Web pages, interest group listservs, library catalogs, FTP sites, Internet services, Gopher servers, electronic journals, and newsletters. Includes location information to connect with resources of interest. Updated weekly. Published by OCLC. Part of the FirstSearch collection of databases.

- *Newspaper Abstracts (NewsAbs). A general reference most useful for research in the social sciences, humanities, business, economics, statistics, and current events.* Indexes significant stories in 50 national and regional newspapers, including *the New York Times, the Los Angeles Times, Washington Post, Boston Globe, San Francisco Chronicle, USA Today, and the Wall Street Journal.* Entries cover 1989 to the present. Updated weekly. Published by UMI. Part of the FirstSearch collection of databases.

- *Online Computer Library Center (OCLC). A database useful for research in business humanities, medicine, popular culture, education, psychology, social sciences, science, and technology.* Database includes over 16,000 sources and more than 15 million records. Links to over 53,000 libraries worldwide. Produces FirstSearch databases. Access full-text documents, abstracts, indices and bibliographic databases. Partners with the Library of Congress for virtual reference service. Subscribers are institutions and an individual for a fee. Produced by OCLC.

- *PAIS Decade. A database most useful for research in business, economics, statistics, government information, and social sciences.* Public Affairs and Information Service database includes more than 200,000 records representing articles, books, conference proceedings, government documents, book chapters, and statistical directories about public affairs. Covers the most recent 10 years. Updated monthly.

- *PapersFirst. A general reference most useful for research in the social sciences and current events.* Database indexes more than 580,000 papers included in every congress, conference, exposition, workshop, symposium, and meeting worldwide and received by the British Library Document Supply Centre's proceedings collection. Entries begin with October 1993. Updated monthly. Full text of papers cited may be ordered. Companion to ProceedingsFirst database. Published by OCLC. Part of the FirstSearch collection of databases.

- *Periodical Abstracts (PerAbs). A general reference most useful for research in the social sciences, humanities, psychology, business, economics, statistics, women's studies, and current events.* Abstracts of more than 1,500 general periodicals and academic journals, covering business, current affairs, economics, literature, religion, psychology, women's studies, and others. Included are transcripts of more than 80 news-oriented television and radio shows. Full text of articles from 530 journals. From January 1986. Updated weekly. Published by UMI. Part of the FirstSearch collection of databases.

– *ProceedingsFirst. A general reference most useful for research in the social sciences, humanities, psychology, statistics and current events.* More than 19,000 citations and tables of contents of papers presented at every congress, symposium, conference, exposition, workshop and meeting worldwide and received at The British Library Document Supply Centre's collection of conference proceedings. Lists papers presented at each conference. Entries begin with October 1993. Updated monthly. Companion to PapersFirst database. Published by OCLC. Part of the FirstSearch collection of databases.

– *Project Muse. A general reference full-text database most useful for research in the arts, humanities, education, psychology, mathematics, social sciences, computer science and current events.* Full-text access to 42 scholarly journals in the humanities, social sciences and mathematics including two electronic-only journals: *Postmodern Culture* and *Theory & Event.* From Johns Hopkins Press.

– *PsycFIRST. A database most useful for research in education, psychology and the social sciences.* More than 1,300 journals on psychology and related fields. Coverage is current year plus the most recent three years. Updated monthly.

– *PsycINFO. A database most useful for research in business, education, medicine, psychiatry, psychology and sociology.* This bibliographic database with abstracts is the master source from which the subset PsycLIT is derived. Contains nearly a million records covering the same types of literature, and materials from the same relevant disciplines as PsycLIT. More than 60,000 new records added annually. PsycINFO provides indexes to journals, book chapters and books plus dissertations and technical reports not found in PsycLIT. Journals indexed from 1974. Books and chapters from 1987. Updated quarterly. Published by the American Psychological Association.

– *PsycLIT. A database most useful for research in business, education, medicine, psychiatry, psychology and sociology.* This bibliographic database with abstracts is a major subset of the PsycINFO database. PsycLIT contains more than 760,000 records covering the same types of literature and materials from the same relevant disciplines as PsycINFO. More than 52,000 new records added annually. PsycLIT provides indexes to journals, book chapters and books. However, PsycINFO's dissertations and technical reports are not included. Journals indexed from 1974. Books and chapters from 1987. Updated quarterly. Published by The American Psychological Association.

– *Reader's Guide Abstracts. A general reference most useful for research in the arts, humanities, education, psychology, social sciences, technology, and current events.* Abstracts of articles published in popular United States and Canadian periodicals. Includes current events and news, fine arts, fashion, education, business, sports, health and nutrition, consumer affairs, and others. Abstracts begin January 1983. Updated monthly. Published by H.W. Wilson Company. Part of the FirstSearch collection of databases.

- *Social Sciences Abstracts. A database most useful for research in the social sciences and social work.* Index to more than 400 international, English-language periodicals in anthropology, criminology, economics, geography, international relations, political science, social work, sociology, and the law. Describes feature articles, biographical sketches, interviews, obituaries, scholarly replies, and book reviews longer than one-half page. Book reviews of government documents and letters to the editor are not included. Each record contains a bibliographic citation and library holdings for the journal. Indexing from February 1983. Abstracts from January 1994. Updated monthly. Published by H.W. Wilson Company. Part of the FirstSearch collection of databases.

- *Social Work Abstracts Plus. A database most useful for research in the social sciences and social work.* Subjects include alcohol abuse, crime, gerontology, psychology, public health, social issues, social sciences, sociology and welfare in tow distinct bibliographic databases: Social Work Abstracts and The Register of Clinical Social Workers. Social Work Abstracts contains information on the fields of social work and human services from 1977 to present. The database provides exceptional coverage of more than 450 journals in all areas of the profession, including theory and practice, areas of service, social issues, and social problems. The Register of Clinical Social Workers is a directory of clinical social workers in the United States. It contains the name, address, telephone number, employer, education, and employment history as well as type of practice and licensing information. Social Work Abstracts Plus offers more than 58,000 records with more than 2,500 added annually. Updated semiannually. Entries begin with 1977. Published by the National Association of Social Workers.

- *Sociofile. A database most useful for research in social sciences and social work.* Bibliographic data on the latest international findings in theoretical and applied sociology, social science, and policy science. Subjects include aging, AIDS, alcohol abuse, anthropology, cities, communications, counseling, crime, culture, death, demography, drugs, education, emergency response, ethics, gerontology, health, healthcare, industry, law, medicine, philosophy, planning, political science, psychiatry, psychology, public administration, public affairs, public health, rehabilitation, religion, social issues, social sciences, sociology and welfare. Database combines Sociological Abstracts with Social Planning Policy and Development Abstracts (SOPODA). SOPODA enhances the theoretical focus of sociological abstracts by adding the applied aspects of sociology. References journal articles, dissertations, book abstracts, chapter abstracts and association paper abstracts as well as citations from books, films, and software. Some 400,000 records with more than 15,000 new records added annually. Updated quarterly. Abstracts from 2,300 journals published since 1974. Enhanced bibliographic citations for dissertations added since 1986. Published by Sociological Abstracts, Inc.

- *Sociological Abstracts (SocioAbs). A database most useful for research in the social sciences.* Database indexes and abstracts more than 1,900 English-language journals in sociology, social work, and related disciplines including anthropology, criminology, demography, education, law and penology, race relations, social psychology, and urban studies. Starts with 1963. Updated six times per year. Published by Sociological Abstracts, Inc. Part of the FirstSearch collection of databases.

- *Statistical Masterfile. A full-text database most useful for research in business, economics, statistics, social sciences and government information.* Statistical data published in the United States by international intergovernmental organizations in the areas of population, business and financial activities, domestic and international trade, government programs, health, and other economic, demographic, social, and political issues. Comprises *American Statistics Index, Index to International Statistics,* and the *Statistical Reference Index.* Subjects include international station government and other publications containing these types of data: population, business and financial activities, domestic and international trade, government programs, health, and other economic, demographic, social, and political trends.

- *Ulrich's Plus. A general reference most useful for research in communications, mass media, physical sciences, technology, social sciences, and current events.* Listing of currently published periodicals. International in scope. Access to 200,000 entries of 67,000 publishers and corporate authors from more than 200 countries around the world. More than 127,000 periodicals in more than 700 subject areas and 60,000 serials, annuals, continuations, conference proceedings, and other publications issued irregularly or less frequently than twice a year. Updated information on 66,000 periodicals per year, and about 11,000 irregular serials or annuals and new titles per year. More than 1,600 cross-referenced subject headings including annotations for about 50,000 titles. Complete names and addresses of serial publishers and distributors. Updated quarterly. Published by Bowker Electronic Publishing.

- *United States Census of Population and Housing, 2000. A database most useful for research in the social sciences, statistics, and government information.* Social, economic, population and housing statistics from the 2000 United States Census. Geographic areas covered for various statistics include the entire United States as well as states, counties, county subdivisions, census tracts/block numbering areas, metropolitan areas and urbanized areas. Population and housing characteristics measured by the Census are as diverse as occupation, ancestry, age, and telephones per housing unit.

- *WorldCat. A general reference union catalog most useful for research in the arts, humanities, education, psychology, social sciences, government information and current events.* WorldCat contains more than 35 million bibliographic records in 370 languages and covering information from 4,000 years of knowledge. The database describes books, periodicals and other materials owned by libraries around the world. WorldCat tells which library owns a particular title. The title then can be requested via Interlibrary Loan (ILL). Does not include individual articles, stories in journals, magazines, newspapers, or book chapters. Updated daily. Published by OCLC. Part of the FirstSearch collection of databases.
- *World Almanac and Book of Facts. A general reference full-text database most useful for research in the arts, business, economics, education, health sciences, humanities, life sciences, physical sciences, psychology, social sciences, statistics, technology, and current events.* Non-electronic database first published in 1868. Covers arts, entertainment, United States cities and states, people in the news, nations of the world, sports, the environment, vital statistics, science, technology, computers, taxes, etc. Published by K-III Reference Corporation. Part of the FirstSearch collection of databases.
- *World Bank Africa Database. A general reference for education and social sciences.* Contains over 1200 indicators of macroeconomic and social data on 53 African nations. Covers 1965 to 2000. Produced by the World Bank

Recommended Steps in Conducting an Electronic Database Search

We listed a variety of electronic databases that might be useful. By no means is the list exhaustive. We recommended that you have a plan in mind when conducting an electronic search. The plan should include the following:

- The research problem should be clearly defined. A short concise problem will aid in reducing the number of databases that need to be searched. Additionally, the terms and variables in your study will assist in focusing the search.
- Succinctly state the purpose of why the search is being conducted. Some possible reasons may be to summarize the state of the art, to update a previous review, to learn more about a problem, to provide research evidence to support or counter a view, to provide information

to revise or adapt a new program, to test a new approach to solving a problem, and to verify or refute other research findings.

–   Select the data bases you which to employ. Select from the list of data bases provided to support your research. By selecting major or minor descriptors your databases can be reduced by using major descriptors. Some descriptors, such as the author's name, name of the journal, words that appear in the abstract may be used, as well as a combination of descriptors by using "and" and "or." The connectors increase the number of references that the computer will select from any database. Searches can also be limited by dates. Unless you are conducting an historical study, you will tend to use the most recent research findings.

SUMMARY

The delivery capability for high-speed searches makes computers more efficient and time saving than traditional methods of library research. Computers reduce the amount of time spent on generic details, allowing more time for creativity and concentration on your research. Time saved combined with accuracy and the ability to navigate through the vast quantity of library materials have made computerized systems popular.

The databases we outlined are available in many school and public libraries. In some instances, a fee may be imposed for accessing and using them. Both the traditional type of library resources and the computerized database type are at your disposal. An understanding of how to use both appropriately and effectively is necessary to conduct any type of research.

Both qualitative and quantitative data sources can be easily located within public and private agencies, including college and university libraries, public libraries, and specific agencies in the community serving under-represented groups. Know the databases and websites you use to obtain data for research. You should be aware of problems in documenting information on the Internet and if used, proceed with caution (Carlson, 2005; Hahn & Stout, 1994).

PART I EXERCISES

The exercises for Part I are designed to give you practical experience with six concepts presented. The concepts are: 1) writing with precision, 2) applying the information in a form and style manual, 3) evaluating scholarly material, 4) writing an annotated bibliography entry, 6) using library resources, and 6) using a database.

EXERCISE 1: EXAMPLES OF WRITING

Editing the work of others can make it possible to gain insight into your own writing.

Directions: Below are five sentences that were taken from work submitted to the authors over the years. Rewrite each sentence using precise language and correct writing mechanics.

1. The research will look at the reasons people give for dropping out of school.
2. In examining the research and making an effort to establish a best practices with regard to suspension practices, this researcher discovered significant discrepancies in the literature between practices and research.
3. Recently, mediation and other related forms of conflict management (which is less adversarial then litigation) have emerged as methods for managing workplace disputes.
4. What is educationally essential is collaboration among the educational community concerning voices of authenticity and implementation of the acquisition of the values, attitudes, skills and knowledge from within our community.
5. The process of hiring more officers under the notion "more is better" rests with Sir Robert Peer, the father of modern law enforcement, belief that law enforcement cannot be taught in a classroom, but must be learned on the street.

EXERCISE 2: WHAT IS YOUR FORM AND STYLE MANUAL IQ?

The purpose of this exercise is to give you a sense of how well you understand how to use a form and style manual as well as the type of frequently used form and style concerns. As stated in Chapter 2, all form and style manuals have the same concerns, but the concerns are addressed differently. Choose a form and style manual that is most appropriate for your field of study or designated by your university or organization.

Directions: Use the most recent edition of the form and style manual to complete the exercise.

Numbers:

Directions: Write the numbers in each item below according to the form and style form and style.

1. There are eight dogs and 10 cats in the yard.
2. 50% of the people in the group liked the food.
3. A 3rd of the pages are missing.
4. After voting, 90 percent of the people wanted Wilson to win.
5. She ate ½ of the pie.
6. He won 1,000,000 dollars in the lottery.
7. The names of the participants are on page four of the program.

Headings:

Directions: Following are the headings for the Review of Literature Chapter. The headings are in the correct order. Rewrite each heading for this chapter according to the form and style manual. The words in parentheses tell you the relation of each heading to other headings.

Review of literature (chapter title)

Improving classrooms and schools: what is important (first major heading)

A model for schools and classroom effectiveness (second major heading)

Effective classrooms (a subheading for the second major heading)

Effective schools (a subheading for the second major heading)

Measuring student achievement (third major heading)

Overview (fourth major heading)

Titles:

Directions: Following are three titles for research reports. Rewrite each title according to the form and style manual.

1. a study of the psychological affects of retention on adults
2. blacks in the air: the tuskegee airmen
3. wars in early america

Citations in Text:

Directions: Respond to the following items according to the form and style manual.

1. Write the following citation three ways it could be written in the text of a research proposal or report:
   - Many customs have their roots in superstition. Franklin, 1999

2. Following are the names of the authors of an article published in 1993:
   – Ray Johnson, Michelle Wilson, Spencer Gibbs, Derrick Allen
   How should the citation be written the first time it appears in the text?
   How should the citation be written the subsequent times it appears in the text?
3. Following are the names of authors of two different books published in 1984:
   – Ray Johnson, Michelle Wilson, Spencer Gibbs, Derrick Moite
   – Ray Johnson, Michelle Wilson, Derrick Moite, Mary Saunders
   How should the citations be written the first time they appear in the text?
   How should the citations be written the subsequent times they appear in the text?
4. Three pieces of literature make the same comments on a topic. Using the names and dates below, write the citation correctly:
   Mitch Wilson 2001, Derrick Moite and Mary Kendall 1978; Anne Roth 1987
5. The Association for Supervision and Curriculum Development published a report in 2005. The organization is listed as the author.
   – How should the citation be written the first time it appears in the text?
   – How should the citation be written the subsequent times in the text?
6. *The Miseducation of the Negro* by Carter G. Woodson was originally published in 1934. You are using the 1991 publication of the book. How should you cite this piece of literature in the text?

Quotations:
1. Appropriately write and cite the following quote for use in the text.
   Page: 63
   Author: Louise Wilson
   Quotation: Political analysts do not offer novel concepts and hypotheses.
   Date: 2001
2. You have a 50-word quote you want to include in the text. How would you do this?
3. What is the purpose of three ellipsis points?
4. Explain what the brackets [ ] in the following quote mean.
   All [people] are created equal.

Bibliographic or Reference List Entries:
Directions: Write the form and style manual page number or numbers, and example number or numbers based on the information that follows.
1. You are using a book with two authors. One author has "III" in his name.
2. You are using the fifth edition of a book.
3. You are using one chapter in the fifth edition of a book.
4. You are using a report published by an agency of the federal government, and it is the author.

5. You are using one article in a journal.
6. You are using a dissertation.
7. You are using a revised edition of a book.
8. You are using one chapter of the revised edition of a book.
9. *The Miseducation of the Negro* by Carter G. Woodson was originally published in 1934. You are using the 1991 publication of the book. How should you write the bibliographic entry for this book in the bibliography or reference list?
10. You are using the entire issue of a journal.

Direction: Rewrite the following three items as one complete bibliography or reference list.
  - HOME IN CANAAN; MARGARET LLOYD; 1996; NEW YORK; POST BOOKS; FIFTH EDITION
  - HABITS OF PEOPLE: INDIVIDUAL AND COMMUNITY; ROBERT JOHNS, MARSHA M. SULLIVAN, DANA P. SWIDLER, SR., BARBARA STEVENSON; WHITEWATER PUBLISHERS; PINE BLUFF, ARKANSAS, 1992
  - THE ROLE OF INSTRUCTION IN TEST SCORE IMPROVEMENT; WILSON GIBBS, SUSAN L. BELCHER; AUGUST 2006; VOLUME 83; NUMBER 1; EDUCATION INSTRUCTION; PAGES 284–290.

Directions: Write the answer to the following.
In a bibliography or reference list, you have to include the location of the publisher. This means that you have to indicate the city and state where the publisher is located. However, there are some cities when you do not have to include the state with the city. What are the names of those cities?

Online References
Directions: Write the form and style manual page number or numbers, and example number or numbers, based on the information that follows, for items 1 and 2. Write your answer to items 3 and 4.
  1. You are using the online data file from the federal government.
  2. You are using a report from the United States government and there is no publication date.
  3. What does the word "retrieved" mean in some of the examples?
  4. After completing your research report, you find that an online source you retrieved can no longer be found. What do you do?

EXERCISE 3: RESEARCH LITERATURE EVALUATION CHECKLIST

The purpose of this exercise to provide you with an opportunity to evaluate literature related to your research topic. The checklist *highlights* concerns when evaluating research articles, scholarly books and research reports. It is an adaption of the extensive guidelines developed by Gay & Airasian (2003), Girden (2001) and Pyrczak (2003) as well as information we believe novice researchers should consider.

Directions: Select an article you believe is appropriate for your study. After reading the article complete the checklist below. Next to each question in the checklist make a mark under "yes" or "no". You must be decisive in your responses. In the column labeled "explain", jot notes on the reason for your "yes" or "no" rating. At the end of the checklist, based on your responses you are asked to provide an overall rating of the article meeting the standards of scholarship.

	YES	NO	EXPLAIN
TITLE			
Does the title concisely describe the topic of the study?			
ABSTRACT			
Does the abstract give you a clear overview of *each* of the following: a) researched problem, b) research participants, c) instruments or treatments, d) research design and the findings?			
Research Problem			
Is there a statement of the researched problem?			
Are the issues or background information on the researched problem included?			
Is the significance of the research study discussed?			
Are variables and terms defined?			
Review of Literature			
Is the review of literature related to the stated research problem?			
Are the majority of the cited materials facts rather than opinions?			
Have the materials in the review of literature been analyzed, synthesized and evaluated?			
Is sufficient information given on the results of studies cited?			
Does the author explain the relation of the cited			

material to the stated research problem?			
Research Questions and Hypotheses			
Are specific research questions to be answered or hypotheses to be tested included?			
Is each research question answerable or each hypothesis testable?			
Is there an obvious connection between the research questions or hypotheses and the stated researched problem?			
Research Methods			
Research Participants			
Are the criteria and procedures to select the research participants clearly described?			
Are the number and attributes of the research participants described?			
Instruments or Treatments			
Are the reasons for selecting the instruments or treatments explained?			
Is each instrument or treatment described in terms of what it measures, how it measures, its development, reliability, validity, and administration procedures?			
Research Design and Procedures			
Is the research study design explained?			

Are the procedures to gather data described?			
Are the procedures to analyze the study's data explained?			
Are the limitations of the research design, instruments or treatments, and data gathering and data analysis procedures discussed?			
Are human subjects protection concerns addressed?			
Findings			
Is each research question answered or each hypothesis tested?			
Are the findings stated clearly?			
Discussion, Conclusions, Recommendations			
Is each finding discussed in relation to the research questions or hypotheses?			
Are the findings discussed in relation to the review of literature content?			
Are the theoretical and practical implications of the findings discussed?			
Are recommendations for further study provided?			

Using your marks and notes above, on a scale of 0 to 5 what overall rating would you give the article you reviewed for meeting the expectations of scholarly research, and explain your rating? Zero means that the article does not meet the standards of scholarship, and 5 means it meets the standards.

EXERCISE 4: ANNOTATED BIBLIOGRAPHY ENTRY

An annotated bibliography is a catalogue of materials you have read. Each annotated bibliography entry addresses three concerns: 1) summary of the literature, 2) your evaluation of its usefulness in relation to your study topic, and 3) indication of how you might use it for your study.

Directions: Select an article on a research study that you believe might be appropriate for your research topic. Provide responses to the following items.

Form and Style

Write the bibliographic information for the articles according to the form and style manual you are using.

Summary of the Article

1. What is the research topic of the article?
2. What is the stated purpose of the research study in the article?
3. What are the primary arguments or points that are made?
4. What are the conclusions of the author or authors?

Evaluation of Usefulness

1. Are the arguments or points made in the article similar or different from arguments or points in other literature you have read? Explain your response and give examples by using citations.
2. Are the conclusions made in the article similar or different from conclusions in other literature you have read? Explain your response and give examples by using citations.

Indication of Use

1. Would the article be appropriate for your research study? Explain your response.
2. How does the information in the article inform your knowledge about your research topic? Explain your response.
3. Does it agree or disagree with your point of view of the research topic? Explain your response.

EXERCISE 5: USING LIBRARY RESOURCES

While computers have made it possible to access a great deal of literature and information for your research study, it still remains necessary to go to a library to use some resources. This exercise is designed to acquaint you with reference library resources. As a reminder, some reference resources include, but are not limited to encyclopedias, abstracts, and card catalogues.

Directions: Identify two reference resources at the library that relate to the field of study or discipline in which your study is grounded. Examine the resources, giving particular attention to how they are arranged, the type of information provided, and how you might use the resources for your research study. Describe each based on your examination.

EXERCISE 6: USING ELECTRONIC DATABASES

Databases are useful research tools to explore accessible information on a research topic. It is might be helpful for you to begin to examine the type of information in an electronic database and the creativity it allows you to have as you examine your research topic.

Directions: Using your research topic follow the steps provided to search an electronic database.

Steps to Search:

1. Select a database from the over 60 provided in Chapter 4 that you believe is most appropriate for obtaining information about your research topic.
2. Enter keywords for your research topic that you believe will provide useful information.
3. When you are reviewing your search results, you need to ask:
    a. Are the results relevant or irrelevant?
    b. Did I receive more results than I can possibly review? If "yes", what are terms that could narrow the search results?
    c. Did I receive an insufficient number of results? If' "yes", what are terms that could broaden the search results?
4. Use the connectors, "and" and "or", with your keywords
5. What are the results? Repeat your review of the results using the questions in 3 a through c.

CONCEPTUALIZING AND FRAMING
A RESEARCH STUDY

Through your preliminary readings you develop a general knowledge base about your research interest or topic. In Part II ways to crystallize your research interest or conceptualize your research topic, and the boundaries or frame for your research topic are discussed.

CHAPTER 5

CONCEPTUALIZING A RESEARCH STUDY

The preliminary phases of research were discussed in Part I. Through observations and extensive preliminary reading you develop a broad knowledge base about what needs to be studied about the a particular topic and identify potential aspects of the research topic to study. Eventually you have to move beyond an interest in a variety of aspects of a research topic and decide on a specific research topic on which you will focus. Determining the specific research topic to study is the conceptualizing of your research study. In this chapter what needs to occur to conceptualize your research topic is described.

ABILITY TO CONDUCT A STUDY

A major concern in conceptualizing a research study is your ability to conduct the study you want to do. We will example what we mean by this with a real example. There once was a doctoral learner who wanted to do a research study on the personal views of the United States Supreme Court justices on *Roe v Wade*. While an interesting research topic, the study idea had to be abandoned because it was not manageable and not researchable by the doctoral learner. The doctoral learner did not have access to the Justices and the funds for travel and lodging to Washington, DC. A research topic might be worthy, researchers have to ask and answer honestly four questions before proceeding with a specific research study topic focus.

Questions 1: Is the research topic interesting to me? The chosen research topic should be of real interest to you. A research study requires a great deal of time and energy. All research studies have challenges. Choosing a research topic that is only a passing interest or one that has been given to you will in all likelihood not sustain your interest to complete the study.

Questions 2: Is the research topic researchable by me? You have to have access to data and information. Having access to data has three considerations. One consideration is if the needed data is within your span of control. Span of control is associated with your role or position in the hierarchy of an organization, association, or even a grassroots group. Span of control can also be associated with your access to individuals who have data you need including potential research participants. For example, most education research occurs in school organizations. A superintendent would have access to certain types of data that would not be accessible to a principal. A principal would have access to certain types of data that would not be accessible to a teacher. You have to acknowledge your connection to the types of data to which you will need access.

The second access consideration, and closely related to the first consideration, is authorities' permission to access needed data. Sometimes span of control will not give you ready access to needed data, but through personal relations or organizational mechanisms you are able to attempt to gain access to the needed data. If one or both are in place, and a positive response is given then you might be able to proceed with the study topic. If a negative response is given then you need to determine if the specific site is the only place to get the data or are there other sites. For example, a learner wanted to study the effect of educational decisions made by unwed women who had attended alternative schools during their pregnancy. The school administrator would not grant permission to conduct the study with the students in the school. Through an exploration of community organizations that work with unwed women who attend alternative schools, the learner was able to obtain permission to have access to the women participating in a community program and conduct the study. Obtaining permission to conduct a study in a specific site should be handled early in the conceptualization stage of a study because some organizations have specific procedures to follow to get permission, and the process can be time consuming.

A final consideration is accessibility to the research participants who meet the criteria for your study. Part of conceptualizing a research study is to consider early the type of data that is needed and the criteria for research participants who are appropriate for your study. Most education and social science data will be obtained from people. You might develop participant criteria, and then find that participants are not readily accessible. You might need to reasonably adjust the criteria, or find ways to identify potential participants, or both. One learner wanted to do case studies on the emotional, social and educational effect of retention in elementary grades had on adults in later life. One criterion for potential participants was that they had to be "successful". In his research "successful" meant that they had a college degree. Due to the narrow focus of the specific criterion for participants, and perhaps the social stigma of being retained, a sufficient number of potential research participants were not readily accessible where he lived. To identify potential research participants to meet all of his criteria, including the one for "success", the learner put out a call for research participants on the Internet.

Question 3: Is the research topic significant for my field of study or discipline? Remember that research is to be shared with other scholars, thus making the research a piece of scholarship. As scholarship, research is a building block of knowledge. You have to determine if conducting the research will become a building block of knowledge and how. Just because the topic is interesting to you, and you complete the research study, the topic will not necessarily be a building block of knowledge. When thinking about the research topic, you need to be able to answer the question, "What new information can my study contribute to the understanding of the research topic, and in turn the field of study or discipline?" To say that your study will be significant because the research topic was studied in Denver but has not been studied in Atlanta is not evidence of significance. There has to be some substantive reason for wanting to conduct the study in Atlanta. A substantive reason could be that there are similarities on the topic in the two cities and conducting it Atlanta would determine if similar or dissimilar findings occur.

Question 4: Can I manage the research topic? Manageability of a research topic is based on three interrelated factors.

Factor 1: A team of researchers investigating a topic will respond differently to this question than a single researcher. The broader and ill defined the study the more uncontrollable it will be. The study has to be well focused.

Factor 2: Your level of research skills will make a difference on what you can manage for a research study. The quality of your study is dependent on your level of research skills. If certain types of research skills are needed to conduct your study and you do not possess them then you will need time to develop the skill. Some types of studies novice researchers cannot effectively complete because a high level of research skill expertise is needed. We believe that one reason most universities require master's and doctoral learners to conduct quantitative studies for their theses and dissertations research is because the research methodologies for the quantitative research approach does not require the same level of research skill expertise as the research methodologies for the qualitative research approach. This is discussed in Part III of this book.

Factor 3: The cost of the study is a factor in what research can be conducted. You have to be realistic about how much you can afford to spend to conduct your study. If you do not have the funds will you seek funding for the study? If you do not have the funds and are not willing to seek funds, then you need to redesign the study so it is within your budget or abandon the study.

Should you find that you cannot answer all four of the ability to conduct a study questions with positive responses you need to either refocus your research interest or abandon the topic.

FROM OBERVATIONS TO CONCEPTUALIZATION

In many respects a research interest emanates from what you observe in your environment and read about based on your observations. All scholarly research occurs within a context of issues in a field of study or discipline. Issues are the contemporary debates and dialogues that are occurring about the research topic. They provide the overall context for your research study by providing background information on the topic.

After you have determined if you are capable to investigate the research topic as you conceptualized it, the next step is to identify the issues that substantiate your observations. The observations are substantiated with literature.

Through the issues two things are accomplished. First, the issues illustrate the significance of your research topic. Second, the issues explain to readers the specific context for your research study.

Table 1 is an example of conceptualizing a research study. It illustrates how to move from personal observations to the context of a study.

Table 1. From observations to study context

Personal Observations	Teacher education program mandates were made by the State's board of regents for all postsecondary institutions in the state. At the postsecondary institution where the researcher is working, she observes that the faculty is resistant to the mandated changes. The administrators are requiring only the minimum level of change for program implementation, and are giving top-down directives. The researcher also observes that the manner in which administrators are addressing the change, even at a minimal level is causing resistant behavior by the faculty. For the past six months on the average there are two articles in the *Chronicle of Higher Education* about higher education institutions addressing external mandated changes.
Research Topic	Mandated change in higher education
Contemporary Issues	1. Higher education institutions will have to change because of external organizations and or agencies mandates (Gibbs, 2003; Watkins & Jones, 1999). 2. Changes in higher education will have to be mandated (Moite, 2000). 3. Change in higher education can be impeded because of norms, values, and attitudes of those who work in higher education institutions (Abode, 1999; Saunders & Tyler, 2001; Wright, Carter & Zeed, 1995).
Study Context	Administrators are identified as a key variable in the initiation and implementation of change (Arkin, 2002; Nunn & White, 1999; Randolph, Lakes & Hunter, 2000).

You begin with your observations. Through your observations and readings you formulate a specific research topic. Then you identify the key contemporary issues about the research topic and substantiate the issues with literature. The 5-

or 7-year rule concerning literature applies for issues. Finally, you determine the context of your study on the research topic with substantiating literature.

The context of the study tells readers the aspect of the research topic that you will study. Based on the information in Table 1 above, it is clear that the research study will concentrate on higher education administrators rather than faculty or even external agencies that mandate change.

When the conceptualization of a research study is completed you are able to write the opening statement for a research proposal or research report. Below is an example of a fully developed opening statement based on the information in Table 1.

Opening statement example

An analysis of the literature concerning higher education indicates that there will be an increase in the influence that state departments of education and legislatures have on the organization, programs, and instructional techniques in higher education. Additionally, it is pointed out that external agencies will mandate changes in various aspects of the standard operating procedures of higher education institutions (Gibbs, 2003; Watkins & Jones, 1999).

The expected increase of mandated change in higher education by external organizations or agencies makes it necessary for people in postsecondary institutions to begin to examine their effectiveness in implementing change. External mandates will require people in these institutions to become aware of how the institutional history, traditions, and standard operating procedures influence the change process (Moite, 2000). Observers of higher education institutions contend that the norms, values, and attitudes in postsecondary institutions are impediments to change (Abode, 1999; Saunders & Tyler, 2001; Wright, Carter, & Zeed, 1995).

Although no one person can alter the impediments to change, certain individuals are in positions to influence institutions' responses to change. A review of the change literature suggests that the administrator is one of the key variables in the initiation and implementation of change (Arkin, 2002; Nunn & White, 1999; Randolph, Lakes & Hunter, 2000).

With the context of the research study identified, there are definitive decisions that you will need to make, as the researcher. Using the information in the box, some of the decisions are the specific administrative level that will be involved in the study, the nature of what will be investigated about the administrators, and the number of higher education institutions in the state that will be involved. How you address these concerns and others is associated with framing or focusing the research study. Framing a research study is discussed in the next chapter.

CHAPTER 6

FRAMING A RESEARCH STUDY

In Chapter 5 we brought you to the point of determining the context of your study. In this chapter we discuss ways to frame your study. We continue the discussion using the example topic in Table 1 and in the example box.

STUDY FRAME

We use the word "frame" to create a visual for you. Many authors use the term "focus" for the same idea. However, we have found that learners tend to better understand what is needed at this stage with the term "frame."

Think of your study as a picture and you are going to put a frame on it. When you frame your research study you are putting boundaries on it. As the researcher, you determine the study frame.

The example topic in the previous chapter ends with the "Study Context", which is that administrators are key to organizational change occurring. Now it has to be decided exactly what about administrators and organizational change will be studied. There are a number of ways that a study about the administrators and organizational change can be framed. Three examples are: 1) Administrators' observations and experiences with change in higher education organizations; 2) Factors administrators find contribute to implementing change in higher education organizations; and 3) How administrators' leadership styles effect change in higher education organizations. This decision determines the "study frame."

The study frame is the initial boundaries you put on your study. It was decided for the examples in Tables 2, 3, and 4 that the study frame is administrators' leadership styles and organization factors associated with change.

Note that in Tables 2, 3, and 4 the study frame for each is exactly the same. Your next decisions are on the specifics of what will be put in your study frame. The require decisions about developing a research sentence and research questions or hypotheses. When these decisions are made you will notice variations in Tables 2, 3, and 4.

RESEARCH SENTENCE

The research sentence is one concise, grammatically correct sentence that precisely states the purpose of your study. Tables 2, 3, and 4 contain three different research sentences. Examine the differences among the three. While they all address higher education administrators' leadership styles and organization factors associated with change, the particular interests vary. In Table 2 the interest in is determining if a relationship exists between higher education administrators' leadership styles and four specific organization factors associated with change. In Table 3 the interest is to test hypotheses about a specific higher education administrator leadership style and four specific organization factors associated with change. In Table 4 the interest is to develop an account of higher education administrators' leadership styles and four specific organization factors associated with change.

The research sentence is your first specific statement of what you will study. Also, the research sentence is the first indication of whether your study will be primarily quantitative or qualitative. In Part III we provide an overview of quantitative and qualitative approaches and methods. For now, suffice it to say that certain words in a research sentence will dictate if the study will be primarily quantitative or qualitative.

RESEARCH QUESTIONS AND HYPOTHESES

Your research questions or hypotheses are subareas of the research sentence that have to be answered or tested to address the purpose of the study stated in your research sentence. There must be an obvious connection between the research sentence and research questions or hypotheses. Tables 2, 3 and 4 include examples of research questions or hypotheses for each research sentence.

Table 2. Quantitative research study example

Personal Observations	Teacher education program mandates were made by the State's board of regents for all postsecondary institutions in the state. At the postsecondary institution where the researcher is working, she observes that the faculty is resistant to the mandated changes. The administrators are requiring only the minimum level of change for program implementation, and are giving top-down directives. The researcher also observes that the manner in which

	administrators are addressing the change, even at a minimal level is causing resistant behavior by the faculty. For the past six months on the average there are two articles in the *Chronicle of Higher Education* about higher education institutions addressing external mandated changes.
Research Topic	Mandated change in higher education
Contemporary Issues	1. Higher education institutions will have to change because of external organizations' and or agencies' mandates (Gibbs, 2003; Watkins & Jones, 1999). 2. Changes in higher education will have to be mandated (Moite, 2000). 3. Change in higher education can be impeded because of norms, values, and attitudes of those who work in higher education institutions (Abode, 1999; Saunders & Tyler, 2001; Wright, Carter & Zeed, 1995).
Study Context	Administrators are identified as a key variable in the initiation and implementation of change (Arkin, 2002; Nunn & White, 1999; Randolph, Lakes & Hunter, 2000).
Study Frame	Higher education administrators leadership styles and organizational factors associated with change
Research Sentence	The purpose of the study is to examine the relationship between higher education administrators' leadership styles and selected organizational factors associated with the change process.
Research Questions	1. Is there a relationship between higher education administrators' leadership styles and their expected change in faculty roles to implement mandated change in higher education institutions? 2. Is there a relationship between administrators' leadership styles and their use of organizational

	rewards and sanction systems to implement mandated change in higher education institutions? 3. Is there a relationship between higher education administrators' leadership styles and faculty acceptance of mandated change in higher education institutions?

"Relationship" and "significance" are two words that when used in a research sentence tells the reader that the study will be primarily quantitative. Table 2 is an example of a research study that is primarily quantitative.

Table 3. Quantitative research study example with hypotheses

Personal Observations	Teacher education program mandates were made by the State's board of regents for all postsecondary institutions in the state. At the postsecondary institution where the researcher is working, she observes that the faculty is resistant to the mandated changes. The administrators are requiring only the minimum level of change for program implementation, and are giving top-down directives. The researcher also observes that the manner in which administrators are addressing the change, even at a minimal level is causing resistant behavior by the faculty. For the past six months on the average there are two articles in the *Chronicle of Higher Education* about higher education institutions addressing external mandated changes.
Research Topic	Mandated change in higher education
Contemporary Issues	1. Higher education institutions will have to change because of external organizations' and or agencies' mandates (Gibbs, 2003; Watkins & Jones, 1999). 2. Changes in higher education will have to be mandated (Moite, 2000).

	3. Change in higher education can be impeded because of norms, values, and attitudes of those who work in higher education institutions (Abode, 1999; Saunders & Tyler, 2001; Wright, Carter & Zeed, 1995).
Study Context	Administrators are identified as a key variable in the initiation and implementation of change (Arkin, 2002; Nunn & White, 1999; Randolph, Lakes & Hunter, 2000).
Study Frame	Higher education administrators' leadership styles and organizational factors associated with change
Research Sentence	The purpose of the study is to investigate the effectiveness of higher education administrators using a top-down leadership style to implement a mandated change in higher education institutions.
Research Hypotheses	1. Higher education administrators who use a top-down leadership style to implement mandated change have fewer faculty who accept the mandated change in higher education institutions. 2. There is a significant difference in faculty acceptance of change with higher education administrators who use a top-down leadership style to implement mandated change and those who use a collaborative leadership style. 3. There is no significant difference in faculty acceptance of change between higher education administrators who use a top-down leadership style to implement mandated change and those who use a collaborative leadership style.

Table 3 is an example of a research sentence with hypotheses. Hypotheses are your predictions of the study findings before you begin the study. You test your hypotheses, using statistics, to determine if your predictions are accurate. Your hypotheses are either supported or not supported by your data. When your data do not support a hypothesis you reject the hypothesis (Gay & Airasian, 2003; Leedy & Ormrod, 2005).

Gay and Airasian (2003) identify three types of hypotheses. The hypotheses in Table 3 correspond to the types. Directional hypotheses, Hypothesis 1, state the direction of the difference or relationship between variables, such as "higher", "lower," "fewer", or "more." Nondirectional hypotheses, Hypothesis 2, state the existence of a difference or relationship between variables, without stating the direction of the relationship. Null hypotheses, Hypothesis 3, state that there will not be a difference or relationship between variables.

Table 4. Qualitative research study example

Personal Observations	Teacher education program mandates were made by the State's board of regents for all postsecondary institutions in the state. At the postsecondary institution where the researcher is working, she observes that the faculty is resistant to the mandated changes. The administrators are requiring only the minimum level of change for program implementation, and are giving top-down directives. The researcher also observes that the manner in which administrators are addressing the change, even at a minimal level is causing resistant behavior by the faculty. For the past six months on the average there are two articles in the *Chronicle of Higher Education* about higher education institutions addressing external mandated changes.
Research Topic	Mandated change in higher education
Contemporary Issues	1. Higher education institutions will have to change because of external organizations' and or agencies' mandates (Gibbs, 2003; Watkins & Jones, 1999). 2. Changes in higher education will have to be mandated (Moite, 2000). 3. Change in higher education can be impeded because of norms, values, and attitudes of those who work in higher education institutions (Abode, 1999;

	Saunders & Tyler, 2001; Wright, Carter & Zeed, 1995).
Study Context	Administrators are identified as a key variable in the initiation and implementation of change (Arkin, 2002; Nunn & White, 1999; Randolph, Lakes & Hunter, 2000).
Study Frame	Higher education administrators leadership styles and organizational factors associated with change
Research Sentence	The purpose of the study is to describe how the leadership styles of higher education administrators influence the implementation of change in higher education.
Research Questions	1. How do administrators expect faculty roles to change to facilitate the implementation of a mandated change in higher education institutions? 2. How do administrators use organizational rewards and sanction systems to facilitate the implementation of a mandated change in higher education institutions? 3. How do administrators' leadership styles contribute too faculty acceptance of a mandated change in higher education institutions?

"Describe" and "explain" are two words that when used in a research sentence tells the reader that the study will be primarily qualitative. Table 4 is an example of a primarily qualitative study. Good qualitative research questions will never be phased so the answer is either "yes" or "no". Qualitative questions, when answered, should lend themselves to description and explanation.

PURPOSE OF THE STUDY STATEMENT

When your research sentence is precise, you can write a purpose of the study statement. Below is an example. Writing a draft of this statement can assist you in developing your research questions or hypotheses.

Purpose of the Study Example

The purpose of the study is to examine the relationship between higher education administrators' leadership style and selected organizational factors associated with the change process.

Six factors were identified through a review of the change literature as being critical in an organization's response to change:

1. Staff resistance;
2. Use of sanctions;
3. Changes in staff attitudes, behaviors, skills, and relationships;
4. Staff involvement;
5. Funding; and
6. Influence on existing programs (Benny, 1983; Hollow, 2001; Mantle & Frick, 1999).

Of the six organizational factors, three were selected for the study. The four organizational factors are: (1) staff resistance, (2) use of sanctions, and (3) changes in staff attitudes, behaviors, skills, and relationships (Mantle & Frick, 1999).

Numerous studies have been conducted and publications are available on the change process in organizations, and more specifically in education (Abode, 2003; Mantle & Frick, 1999; Wallace, 2000). However, the research on the change process in education is for the pre-college levels. Neither researchers nor those in higher education have examined the change process in higher education organizations (Bulk, 2001). This study will contribute to the research on higher education by examining how the leadership styles of administrators affect the change process in higher education.

The complete statement of the purpose of a study is placed early in the research proposal and report. The purpose of the study statement is an explanation of three concerns: (1) what you will study; (2) variables that will be included in the study, and (3) the potential importance of your study as a building block of knowledge. In the example above the three concerns are addressed. In the first paragraph the research sentence is provided. The second paragraph is based on the extensive reading about organizational change. In this paragraph the researcher identifies six factors associated with the change process. Paragraph three is the researcher's identification of the specific three factors that will be included in the study. In the final paragraph the researcher considers the importance or research significance of the study.

SUMMARY

A research study has to be framed so it is possible to determine the boundaries of the study and make the study manageable. The framing of a study is based on decisions you make as the researcher.

Your framed study is the first indication if your study is primarily quantitative or qualitative. When your study is effectively framed you are able to decide what is appropriate and inappropriate for your study, and develop your research plan or design. Decisions for your research plan will include the literature you will need, the specific research participants, the instruments and or treatments you will use, the data gathering procedures and the data analysis procedures.

PART II EXERCISE

EXERCISE – CONCEPTUALIZING AND FRAMING YOUR STUDY

The clarity and manageability of your research study hinges on your ability to effectively conceptualize and frame your study. Once you complete these two stages of the research process a goal-oriented, purposeful research plan can be developed.

Directions: Complete the chart below for your research study.

Personal Observations	
Research Topic	
Contemporary Issues	
Study Context	
Study Frame	
Research Sentence	
Research Questions or Hypotheses	

PART III

RESEARCH APPROACHES

Education research and social science research are a combination of quantitative and qualitative research approaches. However, one of the two approaches is the primary one. Whether the approach is primarily quantitative or qualitative depends on the research sentence and the research questions or hypotheses. Once the study is framed you are able to determine if your study is primarily quantitative or qualitative. When you make that determination you can identify the appropriate research methodology. In this section, general characteristics of quantitative and qualitative research approaches are compared and discussed.

CHAPTER 7

COMPARATIVE OVERVIEW OF QUANTITATIVE AND QUALITATIVE RESEARCH APPROACHES

INTRODUCTION

Research purposes and the type of data sought vary from study to study. All research incorporates aspects of both quantitative and qualitative approaches; however, one approach tends to be primary in a study. For example, in a quantitative study your conclusions and interpretations will be narrative descriptions of the results of the statistical analysis. In a qualitative study you might use descriptive statistics to calculate, for example, the number of times or frequency you identify an idea, occurrence or statement in the data you gathered through your interviews or observations.

The two examples above are basic explanations of using aspects of both approaches in a research study. There are times when it is appropriate to integrate methodologies from both approaches in a study. This is called "mix method." We do not discuss mix method in this book. There are sources that explain the purpose and procedures. Three of the sources are Creswell's *Research Design: Qualitative and Quantitative Approaches*, 2nd edition (2002), Johnson and Christensen's *Educational Research: Quantitative, Qualitative, and Mixed Approaches* 2nd edition (2004) and Patton's *Qualitative Research and Evaluation Methods*, 3rd edition (2002).

You should not conclude that one research approach or its methods are superior to the other. Both approaches have been used to make important contributions to our knowledge and understanding of the human condition. As the researcher, your concern is to determine the appropriate approach and ultimately the method that will enable you to answer your research questions or test your hypotheses.

Creswell (2002) outlines five criteria to consider when selecting a quantitative or a qualitative research design:

- Your worldview as a researcher;
- Your training and experience as a researcher;
- Your psychological attributes;
- Nature of your research problem; and
- Audience for your study (p.9-11).

Creswell explains that a worldview is the researcher's "outlook" of the world. If you prefer to engage in research where the data are subjective and you want to have a close affiliation with the research participants, then your world-view is more qualitative. If you prefer to engage in research where the data are standardized or objective, and you want a detached relationship with the research participants, then your worldview is quantitative. He emphasizes that while you may favor one worldview, your training and experience as a researcher may determine your research approach for a particular study at a given time. The psychological attributes entail your preference for structure, established rules and procedures and a shorter time to conduct the study, which is quantitative; compared to your tolerance for ambiguity of procedures, reliance on your ability to handle "open and emerging" patterns, and a willingness to invest time in a long term study. Finally, Creswell stresses the need for the research approach you choose to be one that will be understood by your audience and compatible with their worldview of research approaches and methods.

SIMILIARITIES AND DIFFERENCES BETWEEN TWO REACHEARCH APPROACHES

Similarities

Quantitative and qualitative research approaches have four similarities. First, they are both used to solve researchable problems and expand knowledge. They both are concerned with reliability and validity of data although they address this concern differently. Both approaches require an extensive use of literature. The researcher gathers, analyzes and interpret data.

Differences

As you might have suspected, there are more differences than similarities between quantitative and qualitative research approaches. Table 6 presents eight points of comparison between the two. The information in Table 6 is the result of our analysis of the work of several authors including Biddle and Anderson (1986), Creswell (2002), Gall et al. (2002), Gay and Eurasian (2003), Leedey and Ormond (2004), Ocher (2005), Patten (2005), Patton (2002), Taylor (2000), and Shank (1993).

Table 6. Differences between quantitative and qualitative research approaches

	Quantitative	Qualitative
Definition	The collection of data to explain phenomena numerically	The collection of data to provide narrative descriptions of phenomena
Reasoning	Deductive – Thinking from the generally known	Inductive – Thinking from the specific to the

	to specific statements, according to some established rules of logic.	general. Researcher's observations and findings formulate the rationale for procedures and conclusions
Key Emphasis	Positivist; Controlled research setting; Researcher isolates parts to study	Naturalistic; Research participants' setting is not controlled; Researcher tries to under and explain the whole
Assumption	Human behavior and experiences can be expressed with numbers	Human behaviors and experiences need to be described with words
Data Gathering Procedures	Standardized	Initially exploratory. It is reflexive, emerging, and open ended
Nature of Data Analysis	Statistical	Descriptive
Characteristics	1. Research is conducted using identified measurements 2. Objective to control for bias and ability to replicate procedures 3. Little weight is placed on values of research participants or the phenomena being studied. 4. Representative sample; employ random sample techniques 5. Literature is reviewed at the beginning of the study to guide the development of research questions or	1. Research measurements are unknown, they emerge 2. Subjective to obtain personal data 3. Value laden 4. Small non-representative sample; no randomization; select individual to participate 5. Literature is reviewed at the beginning of the study to frame the problem, and justify the study.

		hypotheses	
Researcher's Skills	1. Independent from what is being studied and the research participants. 2. Needs technical writing and statistical skills. 3. Comfortable with rules and guidelines for conducting research, low tolerance for ambiguity.		1. Intimately involved and freely interacts with what is being studied and the research participants. 2. Needs literary writing and text analysis skills. 3. Comfortable with lack of specific rules and procedures for conducting research, high tolerance for ambiguity.

In Chapters 8 and 9 we discuss individually the definitions, characteristics and sample methodologies associated with quantitative and qualitative research approaches.

CHAPTER 8

QUANTITATIVE RESEARCH APPROACH

OVERVIEW

Some research designs emphasize gathering numerical data and focusing on numbers. They are typically identified as quantitative research methods. The purpose of quantitative research is to make valid and objective descriptions of phenomena through the use of numbers. Researchers' objectivity is foremost in the design of quantitative research (Hathaway, 1995; Orcher, 2005).

Quantitative methods are derived from the natural sciences. They are designed to ensure that results are objective, reliable, and generalizable to a population. As such quantitative research calls for the use of precise definitions, standardized measures, and objective data collection and analysis methods that are replicable (Taylor, 2000).

Quantitative researchers attempt to show how manipulating the variables can control phenomena, achieve objectivity by not letting their personal biases influence the data collection, analysis and interpretation, and generalize the findings to a population. Personal contact by the researcher with subjects is kept at a minimum. Researchers are considered to be external to the study. Quantitative researchers seek to understand phenomena by isolating and examining the interrelationship among and between variables in a controlled setting (Creswell, 2002; Gay & Airasian, 2003; Lieblich, Tuval-Mashiach, & Zilber, 2003; Orcher, 2005; Patten 2005).

A notable limitation of quantitative research is that it does not recognize the affects of human behaviors and or conditions. Put another way, quantitative research methods do not address the full range of problems in education and the social sciences as well as they do in the natural sciences. This is because complete control and objectivity cannot be successfully achieved in education and the social sciences.

SAMPLES OF QUANTITATIVE RESEARCH METHODS

Quantitative research methods include causal-comparative, correlation, experimental, meta-analysis and quasi-experimental. Following is a brief explanation of each.

Casual-Comparative

Casual-comparative research method, also known as ex post factor research, is used to show cause-and-effect relationships or causality. It is not an experimental method. The method is used when researchers are working with designated groups and cannot manipulate the independent variable because the event has already occurred. Researchers are attempting to discover how one variable influences another one. They are chiefly concerned with the factors that produced the cause-effect condition. Causal-comparative research should be used when the cause cannot be manipulated and researchers are simply trying to establish cause-effect relationship (Best, 2005; Gay & Airasian, 2003). In essence, causal-comparative research yields data that may be used to predict, modify, and change directions and approaches in a program or setting.

Two examples of casual-comparative studies are:
- The effect of growing up in high crime areas on the incarceration rate of teenage girls.
- The effect of early language development of black males on future school success.

Correlation Research

Correlation research is used when researchers want to explore the relationship between two or more continuous variables. Researchers do not manipulate variables. Therefore, the research is not experimental. The relationships are classified as negative or positive and tend to show strong or weak relationships. These relationships assist researchers in explaining, controlling, and predicting phenomena (Gay & Airasian, 2003). Correlations do not show cause and effect. They simply indicate whether relationships occur between two or more variables, and the strength of the relationships. The method permits researchers to analyze several variables at once or a combination of variables to determine how they are related.

Two examples of correlation research are:
- The relationship between teachers and parents having similar concepts of schooling and student achievement.
- The relationship between phonics and reading proficiency.

Experimental Research

Experimental research follows the scientific method more closely than any other research method. Conditions are rigorously controlled. Experimental research can be used when it is possible to both randomly select subjects and randomly assign them to experimental or control groups. Researchers are able to manipulate the experimental variables. Experimental research describes what will be when conditions are scientifically controlled (Gall, Gall & Borg, 2004; Patten, 2005).

Direct manipulation of the independent variable and control of extraneous variables are necessary when conducting experimental research. Attempts are made to keep constant all variables with the exception of the independent variable. Extraneous variables must be controlled so that researchers will be able to determine to what degree the independent variable is related to the dependent variable. Differences in the variation of the independent variable must be noted and researchers must have the flexibility to manipulate and control the time that the subjects are exposed to the independent variable (Gall, Gall & Borg, 2004; Gay & Airasian, 2003; Patten, 2005).

Experimental studies enable the researcher to determine cause-effect. The difference between it and causal-comparative is that the researcher can control the independent variable in experimental research.

Two examples of experimental studies are:
- The effects of massive dosages of Vitamin C on reducing colds.
- The effect of only watching television news on people's understanding of world issues.

Meta-Analysis Research

Some research topics have had several studies conducted about them. As a researcher, you might be interested in summarizing the results and identifying the average or norm findings of studies that were conducted on the research topic. Meta-analysis enables you to do this (Gay & Airasian, 2003; Leedy & Ormrod, 2005).

Meta-analysis requires you to systematically conduct an extensive literature search and review of research studies on the topic, and "convert each study's results to a common statistical index" (Leedy & Ormrod, 2005, p. 273).

Two examples of meta-analysis research are:
- The use of mathematics manipulatives and the application mathematical concepts.
- The three most identified negative side effects of hypertension medication regardless of gender.

Quasi-Experimental Research

It is not always possible to randomly assign research participants to a group. Research conducted in schools is one example of this research constraint. When this situation arises, a quasi-experimental design is used.

Campbell and Stanley (1963) wrote the seminal work on quasi-experimental design. They gave two cautions on using quasi-experimental research designs. First, it should only be used when it is absolutely impossible to do an experimental research design. Second, the researcher must be able to determine which variables are not being controlled. More recent publications that discuses the types of quasi-experimental research designs are Gay and Airasian's *Educational Research: Competencies for Analysis and Applications*, 7th edition (2003), Leedy and Ormrod's *Practical Research: Planning and Design*, 8th edition (2005), and Orcher's *Conducting Research: Social and Behavioral Science Methods* (2005).

Two examples of quasi-experimental research:

- Comparing the scores of high school students in advanced physics at two different schools.
- The effect of involvement in a weight loss program on maintaining weight loss for a year.

STATISTICS

Statistics, a type of mathematics, is basis for analysis in quantitative research (Elmore & Woehlke, 1997). The major goal of statistics is to answer questions or test hypotheses about both human and non-human phenomena by employing sets of numbers in order to make inferences and predictions concerning the behaviors (Harris, 1997; Kirk, 1998; Salkind, 2003).

Characteristics of Statistics

Statistics enable you to accumulate, describe, classify and evaluate experiences and phenomena in an objective manner. It has five general characteristics:

- Statistics aids you by setting up procedures for assembling data, recording it properly, and classifying it so that individual facts may be integrated into like-characterized masses of data.
- Statistics helps you to order and extract whatever knowledge, generalizations, and conclusions may justifiably be drawn from them.
- Statistics is used to describe a large body of data in terms of its essential inherent characteristics. Three main functions of statistics are: description, generalization, and measurement of relationships.
- Statistics is used to generalize when knowledge about a large population is based on limited observations of a small portion of it. Statistics help you determine when generalizations are sound and how far it is permissible to interpret them.
- Statistics is used to determine whether there is any relationship between two or more variables that are present in a situation and, if there is, the magnitude of the relationship.

Statistical Software Packages

The use of computers to analyze data has greatly improved over the last two decades. There is highly reliable software available to accomplish the task of data analysis. These software packages are relatively inexpensive and user friendly. You can save considerable time by using computerized statistical packages, provided that instructions are systematically followed.

Should you decide to use a statistical software package you will still need knowledge of statistics and statistical analysis to adequately interpret the data generated (Thorndike & Dinnel, 2001). The computer can only present the results; not analyze *and* interpret them. Both parametric and non-parametric tests of significance may be analyzed through the use of the computer software packages.

The computer is not a "cure all" for data analysis (Patton, 2002). The computer can complete many of the mechanical details. However, you must select the appropriate computer software, code the data, determine how the data will be recorded on the data sheet, and what things go together to form categories and themes, just to name a few (Heise, 1988; Peck, Devore & Olsen, 2004).

Patton (2002) indicates that computer analysis might not be for everyone and may interfere with the analysis process. Choosing to use a statistical software package is a matter of individual style.

There are numerous statistical packages. We provide five examples below. The first four are free and can be obtained online.

- Dataplot – Conducts statistical analysis and nonlinear modeling, with extensive mathematical and graphical capabilities.
- LISREL – Conducts multilevel analysis for two- and three-level models. Principal component analysis, and exploratory factor analysis. It can handle up to 12 observed variable. A tutorial is provided.
- SIAS – Conducts several types of statistical calculations while on the Internet. A tutorial is provided.
- G*Power – Conducts analysis for t-tests, F-tests, Chi square tests. Computes power, sample sizes, alpha, beta and alpha/beta ratios.
- SPSS – Conducts a broad range of statistical analysis options. One of the most frequently used statistical packages; many university libraries have a site license.

Each of the statistical packages listed can analyze a variety of data. We advise you to review the packages thoroughly to determine which will best perform the type of statistical procedures you desire.

SUMMARY

Quantitative research methods are derived for the natural sciences. They are designed to ensure that results are objective, reliable, valid and generalizable to a specified population and analysis is deductive.

Quantitative research methods yield numerical data. The data are evaluated by using descriptive or inferential statistics. Statistical treatments of data are used to test hypotheses or answer questions.

CHAPTER 9

QUALITATIVE RESEARCH APPROACH

OVERVIEW

Qualitative research methods were initially developed in the social sciences to enable researchers to study social and cultural phenomena and to analyze their complex context. They are designed to reveal participants' behaviors, and the perceptions that influence them with reference to social and cultural issues. Qualitative research is descriptive and the approach is inductive. A variety of empirical data is used and collected (Berg, 2003; Denzin & Lincoln, 2005; Patton, 2002; Riessman, 1993).

Qualitative research is conducted in the "field," the place that researchers designate to conduct their studies. Frequently researchers are participants in the study. Data may be collected from a variety of sources including observations, interviews, examining official documents and records. Qualitative research methods generate voluminous raw data for the researchers to organize, analyze and interpret.

Keeping careful records of interviews and observations control reliability. Validity is not as easily obtained as in quantitative methods. There are processes researchers use to test for validity of data sources (Kirk & Miller, 1999). These include, but are not limited to, (1) using multiple sources to validate information (e.g., to validate interview information through observations); (2) having participants review information for accuracy; and (3) reporting only what the researcher observed and was told, rather than inferring what was believed to have been told or researchers drawing their own conclusions.

Maxwell (1996) identifies three types of validity concerns in qualitative research. What he calls "validity threats." Descriptive validity requires accurate and complete data on which descriptions are based. Interpretation validity requires a researcher to refrain from ". . . imposing one's own framework or meaning, rather than understanding the perspective of the people studied and the meanings they attach to their words and actions" (pp. 89–90). Theory validity requires researchers to consider "alternative explanation or understandings of the phenomena" being studied (p. 90).

As a qualitative researcher you are attempting to discover as much information as possible about the individuals or phenomena under study, by providing detailed narrative descriptions of the individuals or phenomena rather than statistical calculations. As a result, you usually study small groups, and sample size is not a prerequisite.

The greatest limitation of qualitative research is with the level of your research skill expertise. Qualitative research requires more advanced research skills than quantitative. The quality of the research is based on your ability to bring structure and meaning to large amounts of nonnumerical, unstructured data.

SAMPLES OF QUALITATIVE RESEARCH METHODS

There are several types of qualitative methods. The selection of a qualitative method depends upon the nature and scope of the problem you are investigating, your training and experience as a researcher, the receptivity of research participants to your study, types of participants chosen, and the techniques you employ to address researcher biases.

Action Research

Action research is designed to address or solve specific problem in a specific site by using research methods. Used a great deal in educational settings, action research is conducted to obtain a greater understanding of a problem in a setting for the purpose of improving practices.

Action research entails exploring and analyzing what is happening, and interpreting and explaining how and why things occur as they do. Because action research is imbedded in the change process, this approach favors consensual and participatory procedures that enable people to systematically investigate their problem, formulate accurate accounts of their situations, and to devise a plan to resolve the identified problem (Gay & Airasian, 2003; Stringer, 2003). While the research process is applied more informally in action research than with other types of qualitative research methods, a clear definition of the problem to be addressed is required (Jackson & Achilles, 1991).

Patton notes that action research has a narrow focus for publications and dissemination. The ". . . findings are more likely to be through briefings, staff discussions and oral communications" (2002, p. 221).

Two examples of action research studies are:
- Teachers need to know if the new homework polices are meeting their objectives.
- A church committee wants to know how community groups can use the new fellowship hall.

Case Study Research

A case study is an in-depth examination, analysis and description of a person, situation or condition to understand its complexity within a given circumstance. The case study is bounded by time restrictions and place. Case studies are widely used in the social sciences to solve or to investigate societal problems in their natural settings (Merriam, 1998; Stake, 2001).

There are two types of case study designs -- single-site and multiple-site. Single-site designs can be "intrinsic" or "instrumental." An intrinsic case study is when a unique aspect of a case is investigated. An instrumental case study emphasizes a certain issue for examination. Multiple-site design involves more than one case. One type is called "collective" case study. In collective case study several cases are used to study the same phenomenon. Based on repeated facts from the collective data of the cases conclusions can be made about the phenomenon. The other multiple-site case study is referred to as "embedded". An example of embedded case study research is where the case is an organization but data gathering and analysis from several members of the organization are needed. To conduct the case study of the organization, you obtain case data from each specified research participant in the organization. Data and their analysis from each member are similar to a case study in and of itself (Patton, 2002; Stake, 2001; Yin, 2002).

To conduct a case study you develop selected criteria for selection of a case. The criteria depend on the nature and scope of your study. Validity of the case study is essential. One way to determine validity of case study data is to compare one data source to another data source on the same phenomena (Merriam, 1998; Yin, 2002).

Two examples of case study research are:
–   The professional social adjustment experiences of a first-year assistant district attorney.
–   The effect of introducing information technology on the communications patterns of faculty members at a college.

Ethnographic Research

Historically, ethnography has its origins in Anthropology. Ethnography is a description and interpretation of a cultural or social group or system. As the researcher, you examine a group's observable and learned patterns of behavior, customs, and ways of life (Agar, 2001; Harris 2001; Patton, 2002). Feherman adds that ethnographic researchers examine the meanings of behavioral changes of the group being studied (1997).

Ethnographic research requires lengthy observations of group behavior through participant observation. Participant observation is when the researcher is immersed in the day-to-day lives of the people. Using an ethnographical paradigm you observe individuals in interactive settings and use the data to develop cultural themes and patterns depicting daily living conditions of individuals participating in the study site (Agar, 2001; Feherman, 1997).

Two examples of ethnographic research are:
- The grocery store as a social entity in a small rural community.
- The socialization process of new federal prison inmates.

Grounded Theory Research

Grounded theory research was developed as a means to respond to questions posed by sociologists to understand the complexities of human behavior, which could not be assessed through an analysis of descriptive and inferential statistics and statistical manipulations. Grounded theory research is designed to develop or construct theory related to a concept, a process or an action being studied (Creswell, 2002; Gay & Airasian, 2003; Patton, 2002).

Grounded theory is inductively generated from fieldwork that emerges from your observations and interviews in the real world rather than in laboratory a (Gay & Airasian, 2003; Patton, 2002). Creswell (2002) notes two challenges for the grounded theory researchers: 1) Researchers, as much as possible, set aside theirs' and others' theoretical ideas or notions so that the analytic, substantive theory can emerge; and 2) Researchers need to recognize that the primary outcome of a grounded theory study is a theory with specific components, such as a central phenomenon, causal conditions, strategies, conditions and context, and consequences.

Two examples of grounded theory research are:
- The development of a theoretical framework on the career change process of 25- to 35-year-old Asian American females.
- The development of a theoretical framework on rebuilding administrator-faculty communication after a communication breakdown.

Hermeneutics Research

Hermeneutic researchers use qualitative methods to understand, interpret and make conclusions about humans' experiences within an established context. It originated in the study of written texts, and has been extended to social, work and human processes as well as artwork and other human produced products. Whether it is a text, a process, or a piece of art the concern is to determine the original or authentic intention and meaning of the object under study. Researchers suspend, or set aside, their preconceived ideas to arrive at a "correct" understanding of a text, human process, and human products; thereby understanding the substance and essence of the experience (Addison 1994; Patton, 2002; Schwant, 2001).

Two examples of hermeneutic research are:

- Women's attitudinal change about sex when deciding if to have a hysterectomy and after the hysterectomy.
- Jacob Lawrence's portrayal of the black experience in the early 20th century through his painting "The 1920s . . . The Migrants Cast Their Ballots."

Heuristic Research

Heuristic inquiry is a process that begins with a personal question the researcher is attempting to answer about self. The question is one that has been a personal concern for the researcher. "The self of the researcher is present throughout the [research] process." The researcher comes to understand the phenomenon *and* "experiences growing self-awareness and self-knowledge" (Moustakas, 1996, p. 9).

Researchers must be committed to participate in self-discovery and self-knowledge. Specifically defined research questions are necessary. Heuristic research is a form of phenomenological inquiry that involves researcher's self-disclosure. Researchers and co-researchers have experienced the same phenomenon. (Co-researcher is another term for research participants that is specifically for qualitative research methods.) Researchers attempt to provide an accurate report of explanations and comparison of their own experiences with that of the co-researchers (Douglass & Moustakas, 1985; Moustakas, 1996: Patton, 2002).

Two examples of heuristic researcher are:
- The psychological and social-cultural experiences of Latina women who have never been married by 50.
- The career path experiences of people of color who are CEOs of Fortune 500 companies.

Historical Research

Historical research is designed to portray a complete and accurate description of historical events. Historical research may focus on concepts, ideas, institutions, or individuals. These factors seldom operate independent of each other. Rather, they are usually infused. Historical research follows the scientific method (Gay & Airasian, 2003; Patten, 2005).

Historical research is more than a chronological listing of events. Center to this type of research is the pursuit of understanding "the dynamics of human history" (Patten, 2005, p. 10). Additionally, through historical research you are able to understand the past to explain the present or project the future.

Two examples of historical research are:
- The role of a Fortune 500 insurance company in providing housing for middle-class blacks in New York City during the 1940s and 1950s.

- The psychological ramifications on Japanese-Americans' detention experiences during World War II.

Narrative Research

Narrative research is a research approach where the primary interest is in the narration of experiences and stories of people (Lieblich, Tuval-Mashiach, & Zilber, 2003). To understand the experiences of people over time, collaboration between the researcher and research participants or co-researchers is required (Clandinin & Connelly, 2000).

Four types narrative research are a) autobiography which is a self-analysis about one's self, b) biographical study which is a description and analysis of the life of an individual, living or deceased, written by someone other than the individual being studied (Clandinin & Connelly, 2000; Denzin, 1989), c) life history which reports contributions made by individuals and how those contributions have affected society (Cole, 1994; Cole & Knowles, 2001; Geiger, 1986), and d) oral history which is an accounting of the causes and effects of an event on the life of people as told by individuals' personal experiences (Baum, 1991; Sommer & Quinlan, 2002).

The narrative researcher has to create a study design that effectively answers the research questions being asked and simultaneously takes into account the social, political, cultural, philosophical or historical context for the research.

Two examples of narrative research:
- The influence of Maynard Jackson as the first black mayor of Atlanta on the social, economic and political advancement of blacks in the city.
- Adult Australian Aborigines tell of their childhood after being separated from their parents in accordance with Australian law.

Phenomenological Research

Phenomenology is the science of describing human events and behaviors. Phenomenological research is the systematic search for a description of the meaning or essence of a phenomenon and to obtain knowledge through lived human experiences (Moustakas, 1994). A condition for conducting phenomenological research according to O'Mery (1983) is that no preconceived notions or frameworks are presented to guide the researcher. Researchers are to block out their own personal experiences and remove themselves from the research process.

Researchers' intuitions are important in conducting phenomenological research. However, human meaning cannot be inferred from sensation alone. Researchers must look for the total meaning of the events. All the knowledge of a human experience is in one person. Questions are open-ended (Moustakas, 1994; Patton, 2002).

Two examples of phenomenological research are:

- The experiences of job lose during the apex of an academic career.
- The lived experiences of the baby boomers as the primary caregivers of elderly parents.

QUALITATIVE SOFTWARE PROGRAMS

There are software programs for qualitative data. If you decide to use one, then the same cautions apply for them as with the statistical software packages. You need to decide if the use of a software package is appropriate for you and your study. You have to be knowledgeable about the qualitative method and analysis you are using to adequately interpret the data you generate. You have to select the appropriate software program for what you want to do. In *A Software Sourcebook: Computer Programs for Qualitative Data Analysis* (2003) Weitzman and Miles review 24 programs.

SUMMARY

All research follows a basic pattern. However, for qualitative research regardless of the method the patterns may not be as clear initially as with quantitative research. The distinguishing characteristics of qualitative research, as opposed to quantitative research, are that the research occurs in the natural setting of the participants, the researcher is not removed from the research process, rich narrative descriptions are the results of analysis and interpretation, and analysis is inductive.

PART IV

FINAL CONSIDERATIONS

In this last section we emphasize and highlight matters to round out your general understanding of research and facilitate your transition to detailed research methods books. Specifically, we discuss the six types of research data sources, the purposes and contents of research proposals and reports, and answer questions that we are frequently asked.

CHAPTER 10

DATA SOURCES FOR RESEARCH PROJECTS

Think of the research sentence and research questions or hypotheses as the heart of a research study, and data as the blood that flows throughout the study to give it life. Data are used to substantiate statements you make, as in citations in the text of the research proposal or research report; and they are generated or gathered by you to answer your research questions or to test your research hypotheses.

There are five sources of data for research. They are surveys, structured observations, field notes, print materials, and non-print materials. The appropriate data sources for your study are determined by your research sentence and research questions or hypotheses.

INTERVIEWS

Interviews are one of two types of surveys. Interviews are used when you want to explore responses to items or follow up on research participants' responses. Interviews require personal contact with the research participants. The contact can be face-to-face or by telephone.

Interviews are time consuming for the research participants. Research participants need to agree to the designated length of time needed for the interview, and if the interview is face-to-face perhaps travel to an agreed upon interview site. Therefore, it is important that research participants believe the research topic and the amount of time the interview will take are personally relevant. One way for research participants to see the benefit of the study for them is for you to share the study results. If you say that you will share the results then do it. Your reputation as a research requires you to keep your word.

Interviews can also be time consuming and expensive for you. As the researcher, you have to consider that the number of research participants increases the number of interviews you will have to conduct and the amount of time you will need to interview each participant and if needed, follow-up.

Using Interview Surveys of Others

If you use an interview survey that is developed by someone else, you need to review the survey to determine if the interview items are consistent with the types of data you want to collect. You need to obtain information from the interview survey developer on the validity and reliability of the survey. Validity means that the survey measures what it is suppose to measure and the information is accurate. Reliability means that the survey provides consistent information. For surveys the concern is more on validity.

You might determine that only a certain portion of an interview survey is appropriate for your research study. If this is the case, then you need to ask the interview survey developer if the interview survey can be used in part and maintain its validity and reliability. If it can be used in part, then it is important to know exactly how that can be done.

Developing Your Interview Survey

It might be necessary for you to develop an interview survey. It takes time to develop interview surveys. Your knowledge of the topic through your readings and dialogues with others will assist you in developing your interview items. There are books that can assist with developing interview surveys. Two such books are *How to Conduct Surveys: A Step-By-Step Guide* (Fink & Kosecoff, 2005) and *How to Measure Attitudes* (Fitz-Gibbons & Morris, 1994).

If you have to develop an interview survey you must be concerned with content validity. Content validity is determining that the interview survey measures what it is to measure based on a panel of experts. The "experts" are either individuals who are similar to the potential research participants or people who are extremely knowledgeable about your research topic or potential research participants, or a combination of the two. For example, if the research participants are going to be Haitian high school students who are second generation Americans, then you could identify three to five such students to test the draft interview survey. You complete the draft survey with the panel members exactly how you intend to interview the actual research participants. Panel members give you feedback on such concerns as language, the structure of items, the order of items, and what they thought items meant. Panel of expert members can enlighten you on such concerns as length of time of the interview, interview setting and any other matters that might distract a research participant's full attention to the interview. Panel feedback is the way for you to determine if the survey is valid and what modifications are needed in the interview survey before using it for your research study.

The panel members are not used in your actual study. Think of the process of using a panel of experts as a dress rehearsal and the panel members are understudies.

Researcher's Skills

Interviewing is a skill that you will need to develop. Inflection of voice, facial expressions, or even hand jesters can sometimes influence how a research participant might respond.

As part of your interviewer skills you need to have some general knowledge about your research participants beyond the potential data they can provide you. Part of being a skilled interviewer is recognizing if the research participants need a break during the interview. A good rule of thumb is that interviews should not be more than two hours for an adult. Remember, two hours is only a rule of thumb for adults. You will have to take into account personal needs of your research participants. For example, do you have participants with physical disabilities that make it impossible for them to sit for two hours? Are participants able to concentrate on one task for a two-hour period? We have found that some elderly research participants find interviewing physically and mentally exhausting, and the interview survey has to accommodate this. Researchers have consistently found that the average attention span of a child starting kindergarten is 15 minutes, and increases 3 to 5 minutes for each age. *Qualitative Interviewing: The Art of Hearing Data* (Rubin & Rubin, 2005) and *Interviewing as Qualitative Research: A Guide for Researchers in Education and the Social Sciences* (Seidman, 1998) are good resources for understanding the role and needed skills of an interviewer.

Whether you use an interview survey developed by another or one you developed it is helpful to do a pilot test or test run of the interview survey on a couple of people who are representative of the research participants, but will not be part of the study. This might help you become aware and gain insight about your interviewing skills and techniques, and if they need to be honed and or modified.

QUESTIONNAIRES

Questionnaires are the other type of survey. Questionnaires are used when you are definite about the types of questions you want to ask, the responses you want to receive and or want data from a large number of research participants. Questionnaires do not necessarily require personal contact with the research participants. Questionnaires can be mailed (postal or electronically), conducted by telephone, or done in large groups. When using a questionnaire only the items on the questionnaire are used. Unlike an interview, you do not improvise on the questionnaire items while research participants are completing them or follow-up with participants on their responses.

Sending questionnaires by postal service or administering the questionnaires by telephone or in group settings involve expenses that you will incur as the researcher. These expenses could be cost of postage, cost of telephone if calls to participants are long distance, and cost of obtaining a place for large groups. Also expenses are involved in following up with research participants who do not respond by your initial deadline.

Using Questionnaires of Others

Concerns of validity and reliability are the same for questionnaires that are developed by others as they are for the interview survey. One resource for obtaining pre-developed questionnaires, and to some degree interview surveys, is the *Mental Measurement Yearbook* (MMY). MMY is a reference book in university and public libraries. MMY contains information on pre-developed instruments. Instruments are listed according to categories of measurement and areas of interest. Instrument information includes a description of what the instrument is to measure, how and with what types of people it was tested and used, background on validity and reliability, and how to purchase the instrument. There is a caution with using the information in the MMY. All of the instruments in MMY do not necessarily meet the expectations for research. Therefore, you must evaluate the instrument to determine if it is appropriate for research, generally, and then for your study, specifically.

Developing Your Questionnaire

If you develop a questionnaire you have the same time and expense considerations and content validity process concerns as for an interview survey you develop. Time is needed to develop the questionnaire and test it. Four books that can assist you with developing a questionnaire are *Your Opinion, Please!: How to Build the Best Questionnaires in the Field of Education* (Cox, 1996); *How to Conduct Surveys: A Step-By-Step Guide* (Fink & Kosecoff, 2005); *How to Measure Attitudes* (Fitz-Gibbons & Morris, 1994) and *Thinking About Answers: The Application of Cognitive Processes in Survey Methodology* (Sudman, Bradburn & Schwarz, 1996).

Researchers' Skills

Administering questionnaires does not require a particular skill level on your part. The skill is in the development of the questionnaire. The questionnaire needs to be focused and well organized so the respondents can complete it with relative ease. If research participants decide that the questionnaire is taking too long to complete, or the items are not clear, or the information requested is irrelevant, then they might not complete the questionnaire or give meaningless responses (Cox, 1996; Fitz-Gibbons & Morris, 1994).

Questionnaires can be time consuming for the research participant. Like the interview survey, research participants need to agree to the designated length of time needed for the questionnaire and must see the relevance of the research topic in relation to the amount of time it will take to complete the questionnaire. The personal considerations of research participants for interviews are the same for research participants completing questionnaires e.g., physical, mental and age. In addition, with questionnaires you must take into account the reading level ability and other language concerns of the research participants.

Questionnaire Return Rate

One of the greatest challenges of using questionnaires, especially a postal or electronically mailed questionnaire, is the rate of returns. A 30% to 50% return is considered a good return rate (Gay & Airasian, 2003). Given what is considered a good return rate, when using a questionnaire you need to consider how you will get a minimum number of questionnaires returned from the research participants for your study. For example, you are conducting a study with 20 research participants. If 30% to 50% of the research participants return the questionnaires, then the study findings will be based on 6 to 10 research participants. Depending on the nature of the study and the research methodology you have to decide if the number of returns will be acceptable.

If a 30%to 50% initial return rate is not acceptable, then you have to plan how you will get higher returns. Following up with research participants who do not submit questionnaires by your initial deadline and the number of times you will follow up with non-respondents has to be factored in your research plan. *Your Opinion, Please!: How to Build the Best Questionnaires in the field of Education* (Cox, 1996) and *How to Measure Attitudes* (Fitz-Gibbons & Morris, 1994) provide suggestions to increase returns from an initial distribution to follow up.

DEMOGRAPHIC SURVEY

It might be appropriate to develop an instrument to gather demographic data about the research participants. The demographic data provides contextual information about the research participants. A demographic survey can be in the format of an interview or questionnaire. It should align with your determined data gathering method. For quantitative studies, demographic information is a means of providing human context for the study.

We suggest that this instrument is at the beginning of your questionnaire or interview. It becomes a way for research participants to ease into your survey. The demographic instrument should be pilot tested when you test your questionnaire or interview survey for content validity.

There are thousands of things you might want to know about the research participants, however, ask background information that is essential for your study. For example, you are studying how a state's social service and police departments interact with each other. It would be appropriate to ask about the participants' education levels, years in the respective departments, and position titles. Depending on the nature of your study it might be appropriate to ask them their ages, races, ethnicities and genders. For this study it would probably not be appropriate to ask about marital status or income.

STRUCTURED OBSERVATIONS

Structured observations are predetermined, specific behaviors of an individual or group that is monitored for a given period of time by a researcher. For structured observations you have a checklist of the behaviors that are being monitored. On the checklist is the specific context for the behavior, which could be a brief description of the specific behavior or behaviors that are being monitored. Each time the behavior occurs it is marked on the list.

Before the observations begin you need to be specific about what will be monitored. Any behaviors that occur but are not on the list are ignored. For example, you might be observing the number of times Ms. Johnson speaks to student Sam. The only time you mark the checklist is when she speaks to Sam. You are not concerned with the number of times she speaks to other students. In advance of the observations, you determine the length and number of times observations will occur. You must conduct the observations consistently based on the predetermined times and lengths.

Structured observations can be a data source that is least influenced by researcher bias. Either the behavior is observed or it is not observed. However, the presence of an outside observer of a group could influence how the participants behave during the observations. Therefore, your presence should be as unobtrusive as possible.

Observation procedures and instrument have to be developed. The actual observations take time and the procedures and instruments should be tested first. Three books that can assist you with developing and conducting structured observations are *How to Measure Attitudes* (Fitz-Gibbons & Morris, 1994), *Conducting Research* (Orcher, 2005), and *Observing Children in Their Natural World: A Methodological Primer* (Pellegrini, 2004).

FIELD NOTES

Field notes are the least structured data source. They are personal journals or anecdotal notes of behaviors, events, thoughts or observations that are made with a predetermined frequency over a specified period of time. Through the analysis of the field notes themes or patterns of behaviors or setting situations evolve. Field notes can provide a rich tapestry of what is occurring with people, but require a great deal of time and diligence. Field note analysis requires a sophistication of making meaning of unstructured data on your part as the re-searcher (Emerson, Fretz, & Shaw, 1995; Merriam, 1998; Patton, 2002).

You or the research participants can take field notes. For example, you are conducting a three-month, once a week training program. Each individual in the program keeps field notes about his or her experiences during the training sessions. At the end of each training session you have the participants write about their experiences. At the end of the three months you collect the participants' field notes for you to analyze to gain insight into the training program participants' experiences over time.

Writing Ethnographic Fieldnotes (Emerson, et al., 1995), *Qualitative Research and Case Study Application in Education* (Merriam, 1998), and *Qualitative Research and Evaluation Methods* (Patton, 2002) are resources to assist in understanding the use and analysis of field notes.

PRINT MATERIALS

Print materials are the array of pre-produced sources that can be used for citations and assist you in generating data for your study. These data sources include test scores; routine paperwork of an organization; scholarly and professional publications, e.g., books, journals, reports, conference and meeting proceedings; legal documents; organization policies; dissertations; and correspondence.

The advantage of printed materials is that the information already exists and might be readily accessible. However, it is your responsibility to evaluate the accuracy and quality of the data sources and organize them into a useful structure.

NONPRINT MATERIALS

Nonprint materials are media information that can meet scholarship expectations, including films, television broadcasts, cassette recordings, electronic databases and online journals. For some research, these data sources are appropriate and essential. The operative word in the definition of nonprint materials is "scholarship." Clearly, all films, television broadcasts, cassette recordings and online journals and electronic databases are not and do not lend themselves to scholarship. The advantage of these data sources is that the data exist. The challenge that can occur is that as the researcher you have to provide criteria for them being categorized as scholarship sources and the criteria has to stand up to the scrutiny of others. Scott's *A Matter of Record: Documentary Sources in Social Research* (1990) is a source for establishing scholarship criteria for certain types of print and nonprint materials.

CHAPTER 11

RESEARCH PROPOSALS AND REPORTS

INTRODUCTION

Research proposals and reports are written for the sole purpose of sharing information with others. Whether submitting a proposal for grant funding, conference call for papers, or approval by a thesis or dissertation committee there are specific content that has to be included. The same is true for a research report whether it is for reporting research in an article, book, conference proceedings, a thesis or a dissertation. What we call the dissertation format is used to enable novice researchers to clearly see each component of content that is needed in any type of research proposal and report.

While research proposals and reports for non-academic venues might not use the same distinct format or heading titles, the proposal and report will have the content of the dissertation format headings if it meets the standards of scholarship. Resources that expand on what we present in this chapter include *Qualitative Research Design: An Interactive Approach* (Maxwell, 2004), *Proposing Empirical Research* (Patten, 2005), *Writing Empirical Research Reports* (Pyrczak & Bruce, 2005), and *Writing Up Qualitative Research* (Wolcott, 1994).

RESEARCH PROPOSALS

In this section we provide general explanations of what is expected in a research proposal. The amount of exact detail is determined by the institution or organization that will establish criteria for the proposal.

Research proposals are written to share with readers the intent of a research study and how the study will be conducted. They are written prior to the study being implemented so that appropriate approvals can be obtained. One appropriate approval will be the Institutional Review Board (IRB) of the organization with which you are affiliated. The purpose of an IRB is discussed in Chapter 12, Item 3.

Research proposals require substantive substantiation of its content. Therefore, prior to writing the proposal you have to engage in extensive reading and reflection. Given that the study has not been conducted it is critical that you can demonstrate purposeful, goal-directed, and logical reasoning. Demonstrating these indicate to the proposal reviewers that you have an informed insight about the research topic, and that the methodology being proposed appears to be appropriate for the study. The term "appears" is used because given the ambiguous nature of research you might find that the methodology proposed is not the most appropriate methodology once you begin the study. This is probably most true for qualitative research studies. Remember, a characteristic of qualitative research is patterns emerge and it is open ended.

A proposal presents your best thinking based on what you know about the research topic, the nature of your research questions or hypotheses, and your understanding of the research methodology you will employ. Maxwell (2004) emphasizes the need for qualitative research proposals to have a clearly defined justification or argument for the study to proceed.

Contents of a Research Proposal

Begin the research proposal with **a title**. The title is the reader's frame of reference on the topic of the proposal. The title should be specific, concise, and distinctive.

Generally, a research proposal has five sections. Each section is interrelated. While the sections of a research proposal are similar to the ones in a research report, the primary distinction between the proposal and report is that the proposal will reflect your depth of knowledge about the topic but not your breadth of knowledge about the topic. A research report has depth and breadth.

First section. The research proposal focuses on putting the research topic in a context. In this section you provide the **contemporary issues** of the research topic that reveal its nature, scope and significance. The **research sentence** is included and the **research questions or hypotheses** are listed.

Key **terms** for the study are **defined**. The defined terms are essential variables, concepts, and language, which have a specific meaning in your research study. The defined terms are so important to your research study that they will be used consistently throughout the study. You can begin determining which terms need to be defined by asking, "What precisely do the terms in the research sentence and the research questions or hypotheses mean?" Some terms might have a specific meaning for you in relation to your study. Some terms might have a specific meaning from the literature. For terms that have a specific meaning from the literature, citations are needed.

Well-written definitions are specific and concise. The definitions do not included detailed background on the terms. When writing the definitions of the terms section, think in terms of definitions in a dictionary. Table 7 contains two examples of poorly written definitions, better written definitions and explanations of the problems with the poorly written definitions.

Table 7. Writing definitions of terms

Poorly written definition: Interpersonal conflict. For purposes of this study interpersonal conflict is defined as a manifestation, expressed or unexpressed, of a struggle between two interdependent parties when one or both of them perceives (a) emotional hurts, (b) incompatible goals, and/or (c) a scarcity of resources. **Improved definition:** Interpersonal conflict is an expressed or unexpressed manifestation of a struggle between two interdependent parties when one or both perceives emotional hurts, incompatible goals, a scarcity of resources, or some combination of the three. **Explanation:** The poorly written example begins with a sentence fragment. Also, it is wordy, meaning there are a lot of unnecessary words. For example, since the term is being defined in the definition of the terms section for the study, it is understood that the term is being defined in relation to the study.
Poorly written definition: Educational leadership refers to providing effective leadership for teaching and learning to improve our schools and educational systems. **Improved definition:** Educational leadership is the exercise of authority and influence on teaching and learning to improve schools and educational systems. **Explanation:** You cannot define a term with the term. "Our" has no meaning in the definition. Who is "our"?

The final information in the first section of the proposal is the **limitations of the study.** All research studies have limitations. Limitations do not mean that the study should not be conducted. The purpose of stating the limitations of a study is to let the reader know that you acknowledge deficiencies to aspects of the study scope and or design, but in spite of the deficiencies there is a justification for conducting the study. Limitations of the research design can include some of the following concerns. The list is not exhaustive.

- The scope of proposed generalization of the study results;
- Procedures proposed to identify or select research participants;
- The research methods and analysis proposed;
- The nature of the variables in the study; and
- Procedures for administering instruments or treatments.

The stated limitations will vary from study to study. You do not state the limitations and move on. Once stating the limitations you have to explain how the strengths of proceeding as designed outweigh the limitations. The explanation is substantiated with cited information from research methods literature and related research studies where the design and or methodology are similar.

Second section. The **review of literature** in the proposal is not as exhaustive as it is in the research report. In the proposal review of literature you develop an analytical, synthesis and evaluation highlighting related research and information on your research topic to provide the justification or relevance of the study, as well as the context of your study. It contains classic and contemporary literature to demonstrate to readers that you know the essential information about the topic. The proposal review of literature is a preview of the literature topics that will be addressed comprehensively in the research report.

Third section. The **methodology** section is your proposed research plan. In this section you present your informed best thinking about how the study will be conducted.

You begin by describing your proposed **research participants**. In as much detail as possible, you explain your criteria for selection, and the sampling procedures or other procedures you intend to use to identity and select the research participants. This section can be labeled in one of three ways. If every conceivable person who meets your criteria as a potential participant is accessible for participation, then you have a population. Populations occur in quantitative studies. Few studies, even national ones, use a population. But for some studies it is possible to have a population. For example, if you are interested in studying the attitudes of all school principals in a school district, then you have a population.

The most frequently used label for research participants in a quantitative research study is "sample". A sample is a portion of a population. Based on your criteria for research participants, you use a sampling procedure. The sample is representative of the population. The nature, sources, size and characteristics of the sample are described. The specific sampling procedure, such as random, stratified, or cluster is described. The type of sampling procedure you use is based on the nature of the research questions or hypotheses and the research setting.

The final way to label research participates is "research subjects," "co-researchers," or "research participants." The first one can be used in quantitative and qualitative research. The latter two are used in qualitative studies. The term "co-researcher" illustrates the mutual working relationship during the study between researchers and research participants.

In some studies it is necessary to provide the **context of the study**. This section is not always necessary. If a study is occurring in a particular site and the readers' understanding of the nature of the study is heightened by describing the site, or if a specific policy is a key variable in the study and background on the policy assists readers in understanding the research study, then this section should be included.

The following two examples illustrate the type of information that can be provided in the context of the study section. In the first example, the study occurs in a specific school named Courtney Kendall Middle School. The second example is a description of a state mandated change for higher education that is the focus for a research study.

Context of the study section for a specific site example

Courtney-Kendall Middle School is in the Wilson Unified School District. The school is located in the city of Los Gatos, bordering southeast Dallas, Texas. Los Gatos has a population of 78,200 people living in an area of 7.49 square miles. Chamber of Commerce records indicate that 89% of Los Gatos residents are Hispanic, 10% is white, and 1% is other (2002). Most families live in single-family dwellings. *Wilson County Living Index* (2000) indicates that 85% of the working population is blue collar. They have positions that usually do not require a college education, but do require certain types and levels of work skills. The positions include construction trade, hospitality services, and office support.

Courtney-Kendall Middle School has 3,979 students enrolled in 6th through 8th grades. *National School Board Records* indicate that Courtney-Kendall Middle School is the largest middle school in the United States (2000). The student population is 96.5% Hispanic, 3% white, and .5% African American and other ethnicities. Twenty-one percent of the students are in the English as a Second Language (ESL) Program.

The size of the school's facilities necessitates a three-track year round calendar for students. Two tracks are at school, while one track is on vacation. The tracks rotate every eight weeks. Faculty and staff work two tracks and are off for one. The principal works all three tracks, taking designated vacation time.

The faculty and staff include 5 administrators, 9 grade counselors, 1 at-risk counselor, 1 pupil services counselor, 3 Title I advisors, 1 ESL Coordinator, and 185 teachers.

In site-specific descriptions you provide sufficient information for the reader to understand the environment of the site that could be pertinent to understanding the study.

Context of the study section for a specific policy example

The Standards for Colleges and Universities Preparing Teachers was adopted in 1996 by the State of Wish. From this point on it will be referred to as Teacher Education Redesign, or Redesign. By July 2001, Redesign was to be fully implemented by the 56 Wish institutions that certify teachers.

The standards were written in response to increasing evidence that students preparing to be teachers for a changing society needed a broader educational background in order to effectively do their jobs. The teacher education faculty at the 56 universities and colleges involved were to redesign the governance, organization and programs of teacher education (Standards for Colleges and Universities Preparing Teachers, 1996).

A unique aspect of Redesign was the funding arrangement. Unlike many change efforts which were provided seed money for initiation and implementation, the institutions involved in the Teacher Education Redesign continued to receive funding from the Wish Department of Education after the program was incorporated into the institutions' academic programs.

The new standards required an integration of five areas that were considered of concern to all pre-service teachers regardless of content area or level of concentration: reading, human relations, classroom management, diversity, and analysis and evaluation through the use of diagnostic instruments. The Standards also required that the institutions work closely with schools in the community, conduct follow-up studies of graduates, provide teacher education student services, establish an advisory committee for curriculum design and evaluation that was representative of the areas of concern, and provide field experience for students in the schools no later than the beginning of the sophomore year (Standards, 1996).

The spirit of Redesign was to develop teacher education programs that were comprehensive enough to adapt to the needs of pre-service teachers enabling them to address the changing and varying needs of students they will teach. In order to meet the challenge it became obvious that the Redesign program was to be no small undertaking. The Teacher Education Redesign program meant a total restructuring of the goals, programs, and instructional techniques presently used at postsecondary institutions. The restructuring also meant a change in the roles and relationships among faculty members and the organization of education units in the institutions (Standards, 1996).

In descriptions of policies, mission statements, and regulations you explain the impetus and parameters of these types of matters.

Instruments and or **treatments** are discussed. Instruments can include questionnaires, interview surveys, structured observation instruments, and the demographic survey. Included in the discussion of instruments are the types of data the instruments are to measure, the reliability and validity of pre-developed instruments, and the procedures you will use to construct instruments that will be developed and the test you will use for validity, if you develop instruments. When you describe treatments, you provide information on what the treatment is to yield in relation to your research topic as well as background information on its previous use. If you developed the treatment, then you will describe what informed your development of it.

Data gathering procedures describe the steps you propose to take to obtain the needed data to answer the research questions or test hypotheses. The procedures are a chronology of activities you propose to implement to obtain the needed data for your research study.

In a proposal, you have to provide information on **data analysis procedures** that you are considering once the data are obtained. You provide an overview of how the data will be analyzed naming a specific methodology. It is not sufficient to state it will be analyzed qualitatively or quantitatively. As has been explained earlier, there are specific methodologies related to the quantitative research approach, and specific methodologies related to the qualitative research approach. The analysis procedures are not clear until a specific methodology is named and discussed in relation to the nature of the data you intend to gather. Even though the data analysis procedures in the proposal are an overview, you have to substantiate the analysis procedures with citations from the research methods literature.

In a proposal you must give evidence of **participant protection**. These are ethical actions you will take to protect individuals who participate in your study. Included in the ethical concerns are participant anonymity, and how you will communicate with research participants about their rights, potential hazards to them if any, and what you will do to protect them from harm. This is called informed consent. In addition, you mention where you will keep the gathered data, how long you will keep the data, and how you will dispose of it.

Fourth section. This section of a research proposal is your **bibliography or reference list**. Which you use is dependent on your proposal reviewers or organization requirements. We prefer bibliographies for theses and dissertation proposals because they demonstrate to others the depth and breadth of reading that has occurred, and illustrates the types of literature that will be included in the review of literature for the research report. At the proposal stage, the bibliography and reference list only illustrates the type of material you are reviewing and will include in your report.

Fifth section. The final section of the research proposal contains **appendices**. The appendices section includes a sample of the informed consent form, sample of all pre-developed instruments, if requested a draft of instruments you will develop, when appropriate a sample of cover letters, and documents of permission. Documents of permission could be authorization to use copyright materials, letters of agreement to conduct the research in a particular site or organization, or approval of an external IRB.

Outline of a Research Proposal

Education institutions, organizations, and professional associations sometimes provide proposal formats. In cases where one is not provided, following is a suggested outline for a research proposal with headings. You will need to refer to the form and style manual you are using to determine the correct formatting of headings.

Sample Outline

Title Page
Chapter I: The Problem
  - Introduction (The issues and focus of the study)
  - Purpose of the Study (Research sentence)
  - Research Questions or Hypotheses
  - Definition of Terms
  - Limitations of the Study
Chapter II: Review of Literature
Chapter III: Methodology
  - Research Participants
  - Context of the Study (If appropriate)
  - Instrumentation
  - Data Gathering Procedures
  - Data Analysis Procedures
  - Human Participant Protection
Bibliography or Reference List
Appendices
  - Informed Consent Form
  - Instruments
  - Cover Letter
  - Documentation of Permission

RESEARCH REPORTS

The research report is written after the research study is completed. It provides a complete account of all aspects of the research study as well as an in-depth expansion of some information that was provided in the research proposal. As with the research proposal, each section of the research report is interrelated.

Research reports are designed to acquaint the reader with the problem that was studied or investigated as well as explaining the implications of the research study. All who read your report are to have a clear orientation to the researched problem. Data and findings are presented fully.

The gathered and analyzed data for your research study as well as the reviewed literature all serve to substantiate the interpretations and conclusions that you make in the research report. Data are the evidence that the stated research problem was addressed and the results of addressing it. A research report where merely data are presented and not interpreted is useless as research, and does not constitute a building block of knowledge.

Contents of a Research Report

Begin the report with a **title**. As with the research proposal it should be specific, concise, and distinctive. However, the title for the research report might be different from the one for the research proposal. The research proposal title is informed speculation. The research report title is written to provide the reader with a definitive context for your study. Generally there are eight sections in a research report.

First section. Begin the research report with a thorough discussion of the contemporary **issues** related to your research topic. Provide nature, scope, theoretical framework and significance of the research topics. In this section three questions are answered: (1) What are the debates in the field that relate to your research topic?; (2) Of what use is the research study as a building block of knowledge?; and (3) What practical value does your research study have to what is already known? An example of this section was provided in Table 2.

Next is the **purpose of the study.** The research sentence is provided. In the research report an explanation of how the research sentence connects to current knowledge. The specific research study variables are given. For example, you are studying how administrators effect change in higher education. In the literature six variables are identified as measures. You decide that you are only interested in three of the six. You would note the six variables, and then provide a rationale for including only three variables in your study. The rationale is substantiated based on your analysis of the literature. In Table 6 an example of the purpose of the study is provided.

The **definition of terms** section of the research proposal could expand in the research report. It is possible that as the study proceeded, it became necessary to define terms that did not seem necessary to define in the proposal. Refer to Table 8 for examples.

Research questions or hypotheses that were in the research proposal are listed. Now that the study is completed, it is possible that based on the study results the questions or hypotheses need to be fine-tuned. This is especially true for qualitative studies.

The **limitations of the study** from the research proposal are included. After conducting the study, new insights might occur about the limitations that were not included in the research proposal. Edit the limitations to include your new insights. Additional limitations might become apparent as a consequence of conducting the study. Include them also. The research problem, and research questions or hypotheses tell readers what the research *will include*. In this section you state what the study *will not include.*

When you were conceptualizing your study you might have given thought to groups and individuals who would benefit and be interested in the results of your study. In the research report a section is included called "**intended audience.**" The information in this section is answered and explained by two questions: (1) Who will benefit from the study and why?; and (2) Who should read or would be interested in the study and why?

For example, it is not sufficient to write "psychologists." Psychologists, based on their work setting and training, will have varying interest in a study. A clinical psychologist who works in a laboratory, for example, will have a different benefit and interest in a study than a clinical psychologist who is in private practice. Therefore, the benefits and interests of each audience have to be discussed separately.

Second section. The **review of literature** in the research report is a *comprehensive* review of related research and information. As has been stated earlier, the review of literature is an analytic synthesis and evaluation of related research and information, and not merely telling about the cited studies or information. Through the review of literature, four concerns are addressed: (1) evidence that your study was needed; (2) evidence that the methodology you chose was most appropriate for the research questions that were asked or hypotheses that were tested; (3) demonstration of prior and related research to your research topic; and (4) association of your study with prior knowledge on the topic.

You are to keep the reader constantly aware of the manner in which the literature being discussed is related to your research sentence and research questions or hypotheses. Provide sufficient details about studies included in your report, such as, purpose, design, findings, conclusions, strengths, and limitations. Conclude your review of literature with a succinct summary of the fundamental information that is presented in the review and the reader should keep in mind.

Third section. The **methodology** section informs the reader of exactly what you did to conduct the study and why. For a quantitative study enough detail should be given for your methods to be replicated. For a qualitative study enough information needs to given to demonstrate logic in the emerging methods you used.

Research participants are first discussed in this section. In the proposal you explained how you *intended* to identify and select your participants. In the report you state what you *actually* did to identify and select your participants, including the final criteria for research participants. Depending on the appropriateness for your study, the section is labeled population, sample, co-researchers, research subjects, or research participants..

Instrumentation and or **Treatment** section is a detailed description of the instruments and or treatments that were used in the study. The instrument and or treatment information that is provided in the research report is amplified. You will discuss in detail the development and content validity process of instruments you developed and provide a detailed explanation of how treatments were developed and applied.

The **data gathering procedures** section in the research report might be different from what was in the research proposal. Now that the study is completed, you are able to provide a complete chronology of your activities to obtain the needed data. The research proposal was your best thinking at that time on how data might be obtained. In the research report you explain everything that occurred to gather the data, including those activities that were not known during the writing of the research proposal. For example, in the research proposal you might have thought that only one mailing of a questionnaire and two reminders would yield the needed 30% return rate. However, you actually had to send three reminders to yield a 30% return rate. You would not only state that three reminders had to be sent, but also explain how you sent the reminders and the contents of the reminder. Due to the nature and purpose of this section, it needs to be organized in some type of systematic way of exactly what was done step-by-step.

One way to think about the data gathering section is that it is the recipe for your study. When baking a cake, it is not assumed that the baker knows to grease the pan. In this section, you should not take anything for granted. It is not sufficient to state that the questionnaires were sent. Exactly how were they sent? Were they sent through the United States Postal Service, by interoffice courier, or by email?

Along with replication for quantitative research, there is a second concern of equal importance for both approaches. The methodology section is written to enable the reader to determine if appropriate procedures were used to obtain the needed data to answer the research questions or test the hypotheses. Therefore, it would be appropriate to discuss what was done and substantiate what was done with citations from the research literature or similar studies, when appropriate.

Through the analysis of your data, you know the answers to your research questions or test results of your hypotheses. The **data analysis procedures** section contains the actions you took to examine the collected data. Unlike the research proposal, in the research report this section is *detailed and comprehensive*. Explain everything that was done. It is appropriate to include citations from the research methods literature to substantiate your data analysis procedures.

In the research proposal you provide an overview of the intended data analysis procedures. Sometimes what was intended might not be what is suitable once you have your data. Therefore, it is possible that the data analysis procedures in the research proposal might vary from what is in the research report.

Participants' protection section is an expression of the manner in which you guarantee privacy and safety of the research participants, and your obligations to them as the researcher. Depending on what occurred when the study was conducted, this section might not change from the research proposal.

Fourth section.   Based on the procedures described in the "Data Analysis Procedures" of the previous section, the fourth section of the research report is the outcomes of the analysis. This section can be named **results, data analysis or findings**.

The findings are presented in the order in which the research questions or hypotheses were listed earlier in the research report. Restate each research question or hypothesis, and then present the findings. All findings are to be reported, regardless of how minor they may seem to be. Include incidental or unexpected findings. Be cautious about overstating your findings. Demographic data about the research participants are included in this section.

It might be appropriate to develop tables and figures to assist the reader in understanding the findings. Be selective about using them. Tables and figures should have a statement that explains to readers what you want them to notice in relation to your study.

Fifth section.   **Conclusions, discussion, and recommendations** are where you make meaning of what you found. For the sake of the reader begin the section with a summary of the study. Provide a brief review of the purpose of the study, research participants, instruments used, and the findings from the data analysis. Conclusions are not a restatement of the findings, nor are they interpretations. Conclusions are the resulting statements you can make about the findings in terms of your research questions or hypotheses.

Following is an example of stating a conclusion:

Research question: Is there a statistically significant relationship between the type of higher education institutions and the changes in administrative leadership during the implementation of the mandated change?

Finding: The results of the Chi-square tests revealed there was a there was a statistically significant relationship between the type of institution and changes in administrative leadership during the implementation of the mandated change.

Conclusion: Based on the findings, it was concluded that research universities were more likely to change administrators' responsible for mandated change than private liberal arts colleges.

The **discussion of the conclusions** is the interpretations or sense you make about the findings and the conclusions. This is your opportunity to communicate your insights into the meaning of the findings and conclusions. Through the discussion you explain the theoretical and practical implications of the findings and conclusions; thus, exhibiting how your study is a building block of knowledge. Based on your findings and conclusions it might be appropriate to raise questions about existing theories or practices. Refer to the literature in the review of literature section as a frame of reference for interpretations. Be sure to not overstate the meaning of your conclusions.

Recommendations for further study are your way of initiating the circular attribute of research. In this section you provide examples of additional research that might be conducted as a result of your findings, conclusions, and discussion of the conclusions in your study.

Sixth section. In a research proposal you can decide if a reference list or bibliography is used. A **bibliography** is better for a lengthy research report such as, theses, dissertations and major grant reports. Bibliographies illustrate the depth and breadth of sources that informed your knowledge for the research study. In the bibliography all cited sources as well as sources your read that are not cited are included.

Seventh section. The **appendices** section is the collection of three types of materials: 1) permission and authorizations, such as a sample of the informed consent form, letters of authorizations, and cover letters; 2) a sample of instruments used in the study; and 3) information such as tables and figures that are too lengthy or large to include in the body of the text, because it interferes with the flow of the reading the text but can be useful for the reader's understanding. Materials can also be included in the appendices because they contain information to assist the reader in understanding aspects of the study, but are not necessary for the reader to review to understand the content in the body of the research report. All materials in the appendix section should be mentioned in the text. If you have an appendix that you do not mention in the text, then it should be omitted.

Eighth section. The last section of a research report is actually placed at the beginning of the research report. The **abstract** is the last part of the research study that is written. An abstract is an overview of the entire research study.

Academic institutions will stipulate a maximum number of words for an abstract, usually 350, which is consistent with UMI. UMI archives and makes accessible theses and dissertations completed in the United States. Some other organizations might also stipulate the number of words for an abstract and they might call it an "executive report.". To write an abstract you have to be extremely clear about and able to describe succinctly each aspect of the study to stay within the required word limitations.

Generally, abstracts are expected to have the following content:
- Title of the research report (Not part of the word count.)
- Your name (Not part of the word count.)
- The purpose of the research study. This can be your research sentence.
- Description of the methodology. Include: a) pertinent characteristics and description of the research participants or phenomenon; b) all data gathering procedures, e.g., questionnaire, interview, review of records, tests, etc.; and c) data analysis procedures.
- List of the major conclusions of the research study.
- Highlight of recommendations for further study.

Below is an example of an abstract. The total number of words is 294.

Research report abstract example

A STUDY OF THE RELATIONSHIP
BETWEEN ADMINISTRATORS' CHARACTERISTICS
AND THE IMPLEMENTATION OF MANDATED CHANGE
IN HIGHER EDUCATION IN WISH
By

YOUR NAME

How selected administrator characteristics were related to certain organizational factors associated with the change process when implementing mandated change in higher education were examined.

The specific change that was the focal point of this study was the Teacher Education Redesign effort. Redesign was mandated in 56 public and private Wish colleges and universities by the Wish Department of Education in their publication *The Standards for Colleges and Universities Preparing Teachers* (1996). Administrators of Redesign were defined as those individuals who at the time of the survey were identified as having the responsibility of providing direction for the Redesign program in their institutions.

Four questionnaires were mailed to the 56 Redesign administrators to gather data. Multiple regression analysis was employed to test the relationship between the organizational factors and the leadership characteristics of higher education administrators.

As a result of the analysis, the following major conclusions were made:

1. Higher education institutions tended to be rated high for their implementation of the mandated change when the administrator's leadership style was relationship oriented.
2. Higher education administrators who had favorable attitudes towards change tended to expect changes in faculty roles and reported the faculty accepted the mandated change.
3. The organizational reward and sanction system tended to be used by administrators in private liberal arts colleges. These administrators tended to be task-oriented, have favorable attitudes toward change, and reported no change in the administrative leadership of the mandated change.

Based on the findings of this study, it is recommended that other studies be conducted which would:

> 1. Examine the extent to which the findings are generalizable to similar populations.
> 2. Examine how the organizational factors affect the administrator's characteristics.
> 3. Continue to test propositions suggested in the change literature in relation to higher education.

Outline of a Research Report

As stated earlier, regardless of the format of a research report certain types of information is expected in the report to meet the standards of research. The dissertation format is used in most academic settings because it clearly delineates through its sections, what needs to be addressed in a research report. Following is an outline of the sections that is most similar to a dissertation and thesis.

Preliminary Section
    Title page
    Dedication page (optional)
    Acknowledgment page (optional)
    Abstract
    Table of Contents
    – Headings and subheadings
    – List of Tables
    – List of Figures
Main Section
    Chapter I: The Problem
    – Introduction (The issues and focus of the study)
    – Purpose of the Study (Research sentence and explanation)
    – Research Questions or Hypotheses
    – Definition of Terms
       Limitations of the Study
    – Intended Audience
    Chapter II: Review of Literature
    Chapter III: Methodology
    – Population/Sample/Co-researchers/Research subjects/Research participants
    – Context of the Study (If appropriate)
    – Instrumentation/Treatment
    – Data Gathering Procedures
    – Data Analysis Procedures
    – Participant Protection
    Chapter IV: Analysis of the Data
    Chapter V: Summary, Discussion and Recommendations
    – Summary of the Study

- Conclusions of the Study
- Discussion of the Conclusions
- Recommendations for Further Research

Bibliography

Appendices

- Informed Consent Form
- Instruments
- Cover Letters
- Documentation of Permission
- Other pertinent information related to the study.

CHAPTER 12

FREQUENTLY ASKED QUESTIONS

There are questions that novice researchers ask while they are conceptualizing and framing their studies, or when they initially complete the process. In this chapter we answer questions that arise most frequently.

1. *How much time should I allow for my research study?*
Research is time-consuming. Because of the time and energy involved, you need to be extremely interested in the research topic and highly motivated to complete the research study. You need to be ready to devote large blocks of time and energy to read, conduct, and write the research study. Sometimes researchers develop a tentative timeline for each part of the research process. The operative word is "tentative." For a number of reasons, the timeline might have to be modified several times.

2. *How long should my thesis or dissertation or research report be?*
Some organizations give a page limit. When this does not occur, more does not mean better. The length of your research report is based on the nature of your study and your writing style. The quality of the content of the report is more important than the length. We emphasize that you keep you writing focused, avoid extraneous comments and information, and systematically present your information.

3. *What are specific confidentiality concerns I need to consider?*
Universities and other organizations will require you to submit your research proposal to their Institution Review Boards (IRB). This is done before you begin gathering data for your study. The IRB reviews your proposal to insure that your research design, data to be gathered and your role as the researcher will not cause harm to the research participants.

Confidentiality is only one concern of an IRB. The collective of concerns is called "informed consent". This means that prior to participating in your study, research participants are made aware of the nature of your study, what type of information you will need from them, and what you expect from them, to name a few. They accept the conditions to participant in the study, usually by signing a form. Confidentiality is also the tip of the iceberg on your ethical responsibilities as a researcher. While, obtaining information from research participants is important; how you view the research participants is equally important.

It is your responsibility to address the following ethical concerns: (1) All participants have the right to privacy and be treated with dignity. (2) You avoid causing any personal harm to all research participants. (3) You informed research participants on how their information will be used. (4) Research results should be shared with the research participants. (5) Neither school districts nor their representatives can grant permission for a juvenile to participate in a research study. Only the parents or legal guardians of a juvenile can grant permission. (6) Research participants' confidential information must be held in strictest confidence. To use the specific name of an institution or organization in a research report, you have to obtain permission. If obtaining permission is not possible or not granted then you can use a fictitious name.

4.　*How do I get permission to conduct research at a specific site?*
Identify the individual who can give you permission or facilitate getting permission. Prepare answers to questions likely to be asked about your study by the individual. Find out the proper procedures and means to obtain permission, and follow them. If there are deadline lines you need to meet them.

5.　*Is it better to develop an instrument or use one that already exists?*
The answer to this questions is not "Yes" or "No". Using existing instruments that are valid and reliable can shorten the time needed for your study. But, it is more important that the instruments you use are appropriate to obtain the data you need for your study. If an existing instrument does not meet your needs, then you will need to develop the instruments.

6.　*How do I decide on a research design?*
All research designs follow a basic format. Review several designs. Talk with other researchers about the purpose of your study, and research questions or hypotheses, and potential research designs. Most important, choose the one which you believe supports your research and for which you have the level of skills and or resources to conduct.

7.　*What do I do after conceptualizing and framing the study?*
Identify human and physical resources needed to conduct your research, and their accessibility, before engaging in your research study. This might be accomplished through reviewing similar research, evaluating and assessing your competencies to conduct the research, and consulting with informed individuals concerning your research topic.

8.　*Is there a time period when online resources can no longer be used?*
Prior to submitting the final research report you need to determine if all online sources are still accessible. Those that are no longer accessible require you to identify other resources or delete information related to the online citation. Keep in mind, however, that deleting information could mean a critical omission in your research study. If you have to

delete an entry and the information is important for your study you have to find and include a replacement resource.

BIBLIOGRAPHY

Addison, R. B. (1994, November). *Balint leadership and hermeneutic research.* Paper presented at the meeting of the International Balint Federation Congress, Charleston, SC.

Agar, M. H. (2001). *Speaking of ethnography.* Beverly Hills, CA: Sage Publications, Inc.

Ary, D., Jacobs, L.C., Asghar, R. & Sorensen, C. (2005). *Introduction to research in education* (7th ed.). Belmont, CA: Wadsworth.

Bassey, M. (1999). *Case study research in educational settings.* Buckingham, England: Open University Press.

Baum, W. K. (1991).*Transcribing and editing oral history.* Walnut Creek, CA: Alta Mira Press

Berg, B. (2003).*Qualitative research methods for the social sciences* (5th ed.). Boston: Allyn & Bacon.

Best, J. W. & Kahn, J.V. (2005).*Research in education* (10th ed.). Boston: Allyn & Bacon, Inc.

Biddle, B. J., & Anderson, D. S. (1986). Theory, methods, knowledge, and research on teaching. In M. C. Wittrock (Ed.*). Handbook of research on teaching* (3rd ed.) New York: MacMillan.

Blaisdell, E. A. (1998). *Statistics in practice* (2nd ed.). Pacific Grove, CA: Brooks/Cole.

Bogdan, R. C., & Biklen, S. K. (2002). *Qualitative research for education: An introduction to theory and methods.* Boston: Allyn & Bacon.

Campbell, D. T., & Stanley, J. C. (1963). *Experimental and quasi-experimental designs for research.* Chicago: Rand McNally.

Carlson, S. (2005, March 14). Scholars note 'decay' of citation online references. *The Chronicle of Higher Education.* Retrieved September 14, 2005, from http://chronicle.com/daily/2005/03/2005031402n.htm

Cary, R. (1988). *A general survey of qualitative research methodology.* ERIC Publication ED 304448.

Clandinin, D.J. & Connelly, F. M. (2000). *Narrative inquiry: Experience and story in qualitative research.* San Francisco: Jossey-Bass Publishers.

Cole, A. (1994). *Doing life history in theory and in practice.* Paper prepared for the Annual Meeting of the American Educational Research Association, New Orleans, LA.

Cole, A .L. & Knowles, J. G. (2001). *Life in context: Doing reflexive life history research.* Walnut Creek, CA: Alta Mira Press.

Cooper, H. (2001). *Synthesizing research: A guide for literature reviews* (3rd ed.). Thousand Oaks, CA: Sage Publications, Inc.

Cooper, H. & Hedges, L. V. (Eds.). (1997). *The handbook of research synthesis.* New York: Russell Sage Foundation.

Cooper, P. W. (1993). *Field relations and the problem of authenticity in researching participants' perceptions of teaching and learning in classrooms.* British Educational Research Journal, *19,* 4, 323-338.

Cox, J. (1996). *Your opinion, please! How to build the best questionnaires in the field of education.* Thousand Oaks, CA: Corwin Press, Inc.

Creswell, J. W. (1998). *Qualitative inquiry and research design: Choosing among five traditions.* Thousand Oaks, CA: Sage Publications.

Creswell, J. W. (2002). *Research design: Qualitative, quantitative, and mixed methods approaches* (2nd ed.). Thousand Oaks, CA: Sage Publications, Inc.

deMarrais, K. B. (Ed.). (1998). *Inside stories: Qualitative research reflections.* Mahwah, NJ: Lawrence Erlbaum Associates, Publishers.

Dennis, M. L.(1994). *Integrating qualitative and quantitative methods in substance abuse research.* ERIC EJ 500515.

Denzin, N.K. (1989). *Interpretive biography.* Newburg Park, CA: Sage Publications.

Denzin, N. K., & Lincoln, Y. (2005). *The Sage handbook on qualitative research* (3rd ed.). Thousand Oaks, CA: Sage Publications.

Dereshiwsky, M. I., & Packard, R. D. (1992). When words are worth more than a thousand numbers: The power of qualitative research procedures in evaluating the impact of educational programs and practices. Paper presented at the Annual Meeting of the National Council of States, San Diego, CA:ED 362499.

Douglas, B.G., & Moustakas, C. (1985*).* Heuristic inquiry: The internal search to know. *Journal of Humanistic Psychology, 25*, (3).

Elmore, P. B., & Woehlke, P. L. (1997). *Basic statistics.* New York: Longman.

Emerson, R. M., Fretz, R. I., & Shaw, L. L. (1995). *Writing ethnographic fieldnotes.* Chicago: The University of Chicago Press.

Feagin, J. R, Orum, A. M, & Sjoberg, G. (Eds.). (2003). *A case for the case study.* Chapel Hills, NC: University of North Carolina Press.

Fetterman, D. M. (1987). A rainbow of qualitative approaches and concerns. *Education and Urban Society, 20* (1), 4-8.

Fetterman, D.M. (1997). *Ethnography step by step* (2nd ed.). Thousand Oaks, CA: Sage Publications.

Fielding, N.G. & Lee, R.M. (Eds.). (1991). *Using computers in qualitative research.* Thousand Oaks, CA: Sage Publications.

Fielding, N.G. & Lee, R.M. (2000). *Computer analysis and qualitative research.* Thousand Oaks, CA: Sage Publications.

Fink, A. & Kosecoff, J. (2005). *How to conduct surveys: A step-by-step guide* (3rd ed.). Thousand Oaks, CA: Sage Publications.

Fitz-Gibbons, C. R. & Morris, L. L.(1994). *How to measure attitudes* (2nd ed.). Newbury Park, CA: Sage Publications.

Gage, N. L. (1994). The scientific status of research on teaching. *Educational Researcher 44*(4), 371-383.

Gall, M. D., Gall, J. P. & Borg, W. R. (2002). *Educational research: An introduction* (7th ed.). Needhamd Height, MA: Allyn & Bacon, Inc.

Gall, J. P., M.D. Gall, & Borg, W.R. (2004). *Applying educational research* (5th ed.). Needhamd Height, MA: Allyn & Bacon, Inc.

Galvan J. L. (2004). *Writing literature reviews: A guide for students of the social and behavioral sciences* (2nd edn,). Glendale, CA: Pyrczak Publishing.

Gay, L.R., & Airasian, P. (2003). *Educational research: Competencies for analysis and applications* (7th ed.). Upper Saddle River, NJ: Merrill Prentice Hall.

Geiger, S.N.G. (1986). Women's life histories: Methods and content signs. *Journal of Women in Culture and Society, 11,* 334-351.

Gilgun, J. (1999). Finger nails painted red: A feminist semiotic analysis of a hot text. *Qualitative Inquiry, 5*(2), 181-206.

Girden, E. R. (2001). *Evaluating research articles: From start to finish.* Thousand Oaks, CA: Sage Publications.

Glaser, B. G., & Straus, A. L. (1967). The discovery of ground theory: Strategies for qualitative research. Hawthorne, NY: Aldine.

Glaser, B. G. (1978). *Theoretical sensitivity: Advances in the methodology of grounded theory.* Mill Valley, CA: Sociology Press.

Glaser, B.G. (1992). *Emergence versus forcing: Basics of grounded theory analysis.* Mill Valley, CA: The Sociology Press.

Glass, G.V. & Hopkins, K.D. (1996). *Statistical methods in education and psychology* (3rd ed.) Boston: Allyn and Bacon.

Glassford, R. G. (1987). Methodological reconsideration: The shifting paradigms. *Quest, 39*, 295-312.

Gravetter, F. J., & Wallnau, L. B. (2003). *Statistics for the behavioral sciences* (6th ed.). Belmont, CA: Wadsworth.

Guba, E. G. (1981). Criteria for assessing the trustworthiness of naturalistic inquiries. *Educational Communication and Technology Journal, 29*, 75-91, as cited in Owens (1982). Methodological perspective: Methodological rigor in naturalistic. Inquiry: Some issues and answers. *Educational Administrative Quarterly, 18*(2), 1-21.

Guba, E. G. (Ed.). (1995). *The paradigm dialog.* Thousand Oaks, CA: Sage Publications.

Hamel, J., Dufour, S. & Fortin, D. (2001). *Case study methods.* Thousand Oaks, CA: Sage Publications.

Harris, M. (2001). *The rise of anthropological theory* (Rev. ed.). Walnut Creek, CA: Alta Mira Press.

Harris, M. B. (1997). Basic *statistics for behavioral science research* (2nd ed.). Needhamd Height, MA: Allyn & Bacon.

Hathaway, R. S. (1995). Assumptions underlying quantitative and qualitative research: Implications for institutional research. *Research in Higher Education, 36 (*5), 535-562.

Hays, W.L. (1994). *Statistics* (5th ed.). New York: Harcourt-Brace College Publishers.

Heise, D.R. (1988). Computer analysis of cultural structures. *Social Science Computer Review. 6,* 183-197.

Henkel, R. E. (1975). Part-whole correlations and the treatment of ordinal and quasi interval data as interval data. *Pacific Soc. Review, 18,* 3-26.

Hinkle, D. L., Wiersma, W., & Jurs, S. G. (2002). *Applied statistics for the behavioral sciences* (5th ed.). Boston: Houghton-Mifflin Company.

Hoshman, L. T. (1989). Alternate research paradigms: A review and teaching proposal. *Counseling Psychologist, 17* (1), 3-79.

Huck, S., W. (2003). *Reading statistics and research* (4th ed.). Boston: Allyn & Bacon, Inc.

Jackson, C. L. & Achilles, C.M. (1990). Education reform depends on problem clarity. *Planning and Changing, 21,* 26-33.

Jacob, E. (1987). Qualitative research traditions: A review. Review of *Educational Research, 57,* 1-50.

Jacob, E. (1998). Clarifying qualitative research: A focus on traditions. *Education Research, 17,* 16-24.

Jick, T. D. (1979). Mixing qualitative and qualitative methods: Triangulation in action. *Administrative Science Quarterly, 24,* 602-611.

Johnson, B. & Christensen, L. (2004). *Educational research: Quantitative, qualitative, and mixed approaches.* Boston: Pearson Education, Inc.

Kerlinger, F. N. & Lee, H.B. (1999). *Foundation of behavioral research.* Belmont, CA: Wadsworth.

Kirk, J., & Miller, M. L. (1999). *Reliability and validity in qualitative research.* Thousand Oaks, CA: Sage Publications.

Kirk, R. E. (1998). *Statistics: An introduction* (Rev. ed.). Belmont, CA: Wadsworth.

Kirk, R. E. (1995). *Experimental design: Procedures for the behavioral sciences* (3rd ed.). Pacific Grove, CA: Brooks/Cole.

Krueger, R. A. & Casey, M. A. (2000). *Focus groups: A practice guide for applied research* (3rd ed.). Thousand Oaks, CA: Sage Publications.

Lang, G. & Heiss, G.D. (1998). *A practical guide to research methods* (6th ed.). Lanham, MD: Rowman and Littlefield Publishing, Inc.

Lecompte, M. D., & Schensal, J. (1999). *Designing and conducting ethnographic research.* Walnut Creek, CA: Alta Mira Press

Leedy, P. D. & Ormrod, J. E. (2004). *Practical research planning and design* (8th ed.). Upper Saddle River, NJ: Prentice Hall.

Lieblich, A, Tuval-Mashiach, R., & Zilber, T. (2003). *Narrative research: Reading, analysis and interpretation.* Thousand Oaks, CA: Sage

Lincoln, Y. S., & Guba, E. G. (1985). *Naturalistic inquiry.* Beverly Hills, CA: Sage Publications

Lincoln, Y. S., & Guba, E. G. (2000). Paradigmatic controversies, contradictions, and emerging influences. In N. K. Denzin & Y. S. Lincoln (Eds.), *Handbook of qualitative research* (2nd ed.) (pp. 163-188). Thousand Oaks, CA: Sage Publications.

Litwin, M. (1995). *How to measure survey reliability and validity.* Thousand Oaks, CA: Sage Publications

Lodge, P., & Dianne, S. (1988). *The qualitative dimension.* Paper presented at Northern Rocky Mountain Education Research Association. ED301118.

Lofland, J., Lofland, L., Snow, D. & Anderson, L. (2005). *Analyzing social settings: A guide to qualitative observation and analysis* (3rd ed.). Belmont, CA: Wadsworth Publishing Company.

Malec, M. A. (1993). *Essential statistics for social research* (Rev. ed.). Boulder, CO: Westview Press.

Manen, M.V. (1990). *Researching lived experience: Human science for an action pedagogy.* London, Ontario: Althouse.

Marshall, C., & Rossman, G. B. (1999). *Designing qualitative research* (3rd ed.). Thousand Oaks, CA: Sage Publications.

Maso, I & Wester, F. (Eds.) (1996). *The deliberate dialogue: Qualitative perspective on the interview.* Brussels, Belgium: VUB University Press.

Martinez-Pons, M. (1999). *Statistics in modern research: Application in the social sciences and education.* Lanham, MD: University Press of America.

Matsumoto, D. (2000). *Cultural influences on research methods and statistics.* Prospect Heights, IL: Waveland Press Inc.

Maxwell, J.A. (2004). *Qualitative research design: An interactive approach* (2nd ed.). Thousand Oaks, CA: Sage Publications.

May, T. (2001). *Social research: Issues, methods and process* (3rd ed.). Buckingham, England: Open University Press.

McKay, J.A. (1992). Professional development through action research. *Journal of Staff Development, 13,* (1), 18-21.

McMillan, J. (2003). *Educational research: Fundamentals for the consumer* (4th ed.). Boston: Allyn & Bacon, Inc.

McNamara, J. F. (1994). *Survey and experiments in educational research.* Lancaster, PA: Technomic Publishing.

Mertler, C. A.& Charles, C.M. (2004). *Introduction to educational research* (5th ed.). New York: Longman Publishing Company.

Merriam, S. B. (1998). *Qualitative research and case study applications in education* (Rev. ed.). San Francisco: Jossey-Bass Publishers.

Miller, S., I., & Fredericks, M. (1996). *Qualitative research methods: Social epistemology and practical inquiry.* New York: Peter Lang.

Morgan, D. L. (1996). *Focus groups as qualitative research* (2nd ed.). Thousand Oaks, CA: Sage Publications.

Morse, J. M., & Field, P.A. (1995). *Qualitative research methods for health professional.* Thousands Oaks, CA: Sage.

Moustakas, C.(1994). *Phenomenological research methods.* Thousand Oaks, CA: Sage Publications.

Moustakas, C. (1996). *Heuristic research: Design, methodology, and applications.* Thousand Oaks, CA: Sage Publications.

O,Brien, N. P. (2000). *Education: A guide to reference and information sources.* Englewood, CO: Libraries Unlimited.

O'Mery, A. (1983). Phenomenology: A method for nursing research. *Advances in Nursing Science.* 5, 49-63.

Orcher, L. T. (2005). *Conducting research: Social and behavioral science methods.* Glendale, CA: Pyrczak Publishing.

Patten, M. L. (2005a). *Proposing empirical research* (3rd ed.). Glendale, CA: Pyrczak Publishing.

Patten, M. L. (2005b). *Understanding research methods: An overview of the essentials* (5th ed.). Glendale, CA: Pyrczak Publishing.

Patton, M. Q. (2002). *Qualitative research and evaluation methods* (3rd ed.). Thousand Oaks, CA: Sage Publications.

Peck, R., Devore, J. L. & Olsen, C. (2004). *Introduction to statistics and data analysis.* Pacific Grove, CA: Brooks/Cole.

Pellegrini, A. D. (2004). *Observing children in their natural worlds: A methodological primer* (2nd ed.). Mahwah, NJ: Lawrence Erlbaum Associates, Publishers.

Pickett, W., & Burrill, D. F. (1994). The use of quantitative evidence in research: A comparative study of two literatures. *Educational Research, 23* (6), 18-21.

Pounder, D. G. (1993). *Rigor in traditional quantitative methods.* Paper presented at the annual meeting of the American Educational Research Association. Atlanta, GA: ED 363975.

Pyrczak, F. (2003). *Evaluating research in academic journals* (2nd ed.). Los Angeles: Pyrczak Publishing.

Pyrczak, F. & Bruce, R. R. (2005). *Writing empirical research reports* (5th ed.).Glendale: Pyrczak Publishing.

Riessman, C. K. (1993). *Narrative analysis.* Thousand Oaks, CA: Sage Publications.

Rubin, H. J. & Rubin, I.S. (2004). *Qualitative interviewing: The art of hearing data* (2nd ed.). Thousand Oaks, CA: Sage Publications.

Salkind, N.J. (2003). *Statistics for people who (think they) hate statistics.* Thousand Oaks, CA: Sage Publications.

Schwandt, T. A. (2001). *Dictionary of qualitative inquiry* (Rev. ed.). Thousand Oaks, CA: Sage Publications.

Scott, J. (1990). *A matter of record: Documentary sources in social research.* Cambridge, England: Polity Press.

Seidman, I. (1998). *Interviewing as qualitative research: A guide for researchers in education and the social sciences* (2nd ed.). New York, Teacher College Press.

Shank, G. (1993). *Qualitative research? Quantitative research? What's the problem? Resolving the dilemma via a post constructivist approach.* Presented at the Association for Educational Communication and Technology Convention. ED 362202.

Sommer, B. W. & Quinlan, M. K. (2002). *The oral history manual.* Walnut Creek, CA: Alta Mira Press.

Spradley, J.P. (1980). *Participant observation.* New York: Holt, Rinehardt & Wilson.

Stake, R. (2001). *The art of case study research.* Thousand Oaks CA: Sage Publications.

Steckler, A. (1992). Toward integrating qualitative and quantitative methods: An introduction. *Health Education Quarterly, 19,* 1–8.

Strauss, A. and Corbin, J. (1998). *Basics of qualitative research.: Techniques and procedures for developing grounded theory* (2nd ed.). Thousand Oaks, CA: Sage Publications.

Stringer, E. (2003). *Action research in education.* Upper Saddle River, NJ: Prentice Hall.

Sudman, S., Bradburn, N.M., & Schwarz, N. (1996). *Thinking about answers: The application of cognitive processes to survey methodology.* San Francisco: Jossey-Bass Publishers.

Swanson, S. (1992). *Mixed-method triangulation: Theory and practice compared.* Paper presented at the Annual Meeting of the American Educational Research Association, San Francisco.

Taylor, G. R. (2000). *Integrating quantitative and qualitative methods in research.* Lanham, MD: University Press of America.

Thorndike, R. M., & Dinnel, D. L. (2001). *Basic statistics for the behavioral sciences.* Upper Saddle River, NJ: Prentice Hall, Inc.

Weber, R. P. (1990). *Basic content analysis* (2nd ed.). Thousand Oaks, CA: Sage Publications.

Weitzman, E. A. & Miles, M. B. (2003). *A software sourcebook: Computer programs for qualitative data analysis.* Thousand Oaks, CA: Sage Publications.

Wolcott, H.F. (1994). *Transforming qualitative data: Descriptions, analysis, and interpretation.* Thousand Oaks, CA: Sage Publications.

Wolcott, H.F. (2001). *Writing up qualitative research* (2nd ed.). Thousand Oaks, CA: Sage Publications.

Yin, R. K. (2002). *Case study research: Design and methods* (3rd ed.). Thousand Oaks CA: Sage Publications.

INDEX

A

attributes of the research process, *3*

D

data source
    field notes, *98–99*
    interview, *93–95*
    nonprint materials, *99*
    print materials, *99*
    questionnaire, *95–97*
    structure observations, *98*

F

form and style manuals, purpose, *12*

L

literature perspective
    age, *20*
    intended audience, *21*
    original contact, *20*
literature perspectives, *19*
literature, evaluation criteria, *18*
literature, for comparison, *18*
literature, for conceptual and
    framework, *15*
literature, need to evaluate, *18*
logical argument, *9*

P

purpose of the study, example, *67*

Q

qualitative and quantitative
    comparison, *74*
qualitative method
    action research, *84*
    case study research, *85*
    ethnographic research, *85*
    grounded theory research, *86*
    hermeneutics research, *86*
    heuristic research, *87*
    historical research, *87*
    narrative research, *88*
    phenomenological research, *88*
quantitative method
    causal-comparative, *77*
    correlation research, *78*
    experimental research, *78*
    meta-analysis research, *79*
    quasi-experimental research, *79*

R

research proposal
    content, *102–7*
research report
    content, *109–14*
Research requirement, *3*
research tools
    electronic databases, *25*
    library, *23*
Research, unbiased, *3*
researcher, tasks, *7*
review of literature, purpose, *17*

S

Scholarly research, *3, 6*
study conceptualization, process, *58*
study framework, examples, *61*

ABOUT THE AUTHORS

Cynthia L Jackson, Ph.D., is Administrative Chair and Professor of the Division of Education at the University of the Virgin Islands. She is a former Dean of the Graduate College of Interdisciplinary Studies and Core Professor of the Union Institute & University. She received her doctorate from The Ohio State University in Educational Development: Policy Analysis. She has served as a dissertation advisor at three universities and taught graduate courses. Additionally, she has served as external scholar on doctoral committees. She designed, developed, and for several years taught, a doctoral seminar titled "Conceptualizing and Framing Research: The First Step". Many seminar materials, examples and exercises in the *Primer* are a result of the seminar. Dr. Jackson has conducted and published policy research on all levels of education, kindergarten through graduate, and for non-educational organizations. She is the author of *African American Education: A Reference Handbook* (2001) and co-author of *Historically Black Colleges and Universities: A Reference Handbook* (2003).

George R. Taylor, Ph.D., is Professor of Special Education, Chairperson Emeritus of the Department of Special Education at Coppin State University, and Core Faculty at The Union Institute and University. He received his doctorate from American University in Educational Psychology. His knowledge and expertise in the areas of research and Special Education are both locally and nationally acknowledged. He made significant contributions through his research and publications in the areas of Special Education, Research, and Education. Dr. Taylor has also served as the principal investigator for several Federal Research grants and conducted numerous research workshops and seminars throughout the country.

CPSIA information can be obtained at www.ICGtesting.com
Printed in the USA
LVOW01s0801310715

448216LV00009B/55/P